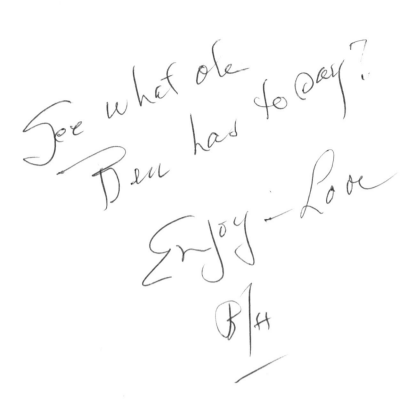

See what ole
Ben had to say?

Enjoy — Love
B/H

Ben Bernanke's Fed

Ben Bernanke's Fed

THE FEDERAL RESERVE
AFTER GREENSPAN

Ethan S. Harris

HARVARD BUSINESS PRESS

Boston, Massachusetts

Contents

Acknowledgments

Why Bernanke? I've always thought I had "a book in me"; that is, that I could bring serious economics to a broad audience. Writing about the new Fed chairman seemed natural. "Fed watching" is arguably the most important part of my job as Chief U.S. Economist at Lehman Brothers. It is a topic of great interest to investors and anyone concerned about the U.S. economic outlook. Besides, there is no competition: there are lots of books on Alan Greenspan, but no books on Bernanke.

Visiting a bookstore in Tokyo in May, 2008, I found two piles of books on the Fed prominently displayed side by side: one pile with Greenspan's memoirs, *The Age of Turbulence*, and another bigger pile with William Fleckenstein's anti-Greenspan screed, *Greenspan's Bubbles: The Age of Ignorance at the Federal Reserve*.[1] Clearly, Greenspan's legacy is important, but the hot debate about Greenspan distracts attention from the real issues at hand. There is a new kid in town who faces bigger challenges than Greenspan ever did and who brings an agenda for change to the Fed. Indeed, one of the big mistakes many analysts and investors have made in the last two years is to view Bernanke through Greenspan glasses.

Why now? It is much too early to provide a final judgment on the Bernanke-led Fed. However, I am not a historian; I'm in the forecasting and investment-advice business. That requires making timely, but imprecise, judgments. One thing I am sure of is that there will be a better book on the Bernanke Fed some time in the future. Until then, views of the Fed are being shaped by narrowly focused op-ed pieces, newsletters and press reports. Seeing the Fed forest for the trees requires a broader perspective.

This book draws heavily on my research at Lehman Brothers, including e-mail exchanges, hallway debates, our weekly newsletter, and a long preview of Bernanke titled "Bernanke: A Guide to the New Fed Chairman," published in February 2006.[2] So I owe a big debt of gratitude to my colleagues in Lehman's Global Economics team as well as the broader research team at Lehman. Lehman Brothers research regularly ranks first on a variety of investor polls for good reason.

I'd like to give particular thanks to Joe Abate, Kenji Abe, Tom Heenan, Drew Matus, Michelle Meyer, Mindy Mraz, Zach Pandl, Paul Sheard, and John Shin, who all collaborated on or critiqued my writings on the Fed. Thanks to Michelle and Zach also for helping with the charts and fact checking. A special thanks to John Llewellyn, Michael Hanson, and six peer reviewers for reading the entire manuscript. This required considerable fortitude, particularly for the early draft. Kirsten Sandberg, Jen Waring, and the rest of the team at Harvard Business Press did a great job pushing this project forward with unreasonable deadlines and perfectly reasonable editorial advice. And finally, a heartfelt thanks to my family—Gordana, Zach and Emily—for tolerating my mental absence on weekends and during vacations over the past year.

1

It's All About the Benjamin

An Early Look at
the New Fed Chairman

The chair of the Federal Reserve is often described as the second most powerful job in America. By pushing interest rates up and down, the Fed can send ripples throughout global capital markets. This jiggering of rates influences the strength or weakness of the world economy and, ultimately, inflation. No wonder nothing concentrates the minds of investors more than a speech by the Fed's leader: just by hinting at Fed action, the chair can make or break a day in the international financial markets.

Yet, the new Fed chair, Ben Bernanke, remains something of a mystery to investors and the press. He slipped into the job with nearly no fanfare. With the Senate focused on controversial appointments for the U.S. Supreme Court, Bernanke's confirmation hearings in the fall of 2005 were largely ignored. The Senate approved him with little debate and only one dissent, from Senator Jim Bunning (R-Ky.), a perennial critic of the Fed. Bunning's concern: Bernanke was too much like his predecessor, Alan Greenspan.

Bernanke's swearing in on February 6, 2006, marked the end of Greenspan's eighteen-and-a-half-year career. The former chair had been both lionized and demonized by the media. Journalist Bob Woodward's book on Greenspan, *Maestro*, was so titled because of Greenspan's dexterity in directing the U.S. economy and financial markets.[1] After the Fed's bailout of capital markets in 1998, *Time* magazine put Greenspan on its cover (with Robert Rubin and Larry Summers behind him) with the headline, "The Committee to Save the World."[2] At the Fed's annual Jackson Hole, Wyoming, conference in August 2005, a paper presented by Princeton economists Alan Blinder and Ricardo Reis noted, "No one has yet credited Alan Greenspan with the fall of the Soviet Union or the rise of the Boston Red Sox, although both may come as the legend grows."[3] The report concluded, "He has a legitimate claim to being the greatest central banker who ever lived."[4]

Greenspan had an enviable record. The Fed had surrendered its most precious asset—its anti-inflation credibility—under the leadership of Arthur Burns and G. William Miller in the 1970s. But, by 2005, with consumer price inflation down to about 2 percent, Greenspan had seemingly won the war on inflation that former Fed chair Paul Volcker started in 1979. Moreover, Greenspan guided the economy through a number of major financial crises and only two short recessions. Historically, recessions had come every five years or so, with the unemployment rate getting as high as 10 percent; but Greenspan managed to flatten out business cycle and hold the unemployment rate at or well under 7.8 percent (see figure 1-1).

Wall Street gave Bernanke mixed reviews. Business economists welcomed Bush's choice—on most surveys, he was the number-one or -two choice on the Street.[5] After all, Bernanke had an impressive academic record—a long string of publications on topics relevant to monetary policy—and had served three years as one of the Fed's seven governors. I considered him the most likely and best qualified among a wide range of rumored candidates.[6] However, many traders and investors were skeptical. They asked, Isn't this "Helicopter Ben," the guy who recommended flooding the economy with cash to counter deflation? Isn't he too academic for

FIGURE 1-1

The unemployment rate

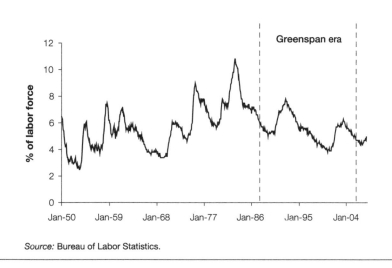

Source: Bureau of Labor Statistics.

the job? Doesn't he lack Greenspan's skill in sniffing out shifts in the economy? More generally, the question was, Can anyone really replace Greenspan?

Meanwhile, to people on Main Street, Bernanke seemed like Greenspan-lite: an undistinguished imitation of the original. Indeed, even a year and a half into Bernanke's term, a *Wall Street Journal* poll pegged Bernanke's approval rating at 12 percent—and a 7 percent disapproval rating. Why? Sixty-seven percent of respondents did not know who he was. (Perhaps someone should write a book about him?)

A BUMPY LANDING

Bernanke not only replaced a legend, he stepped into the job when the Fed was attempting a soft landing—trying to slow the economy down enough to avoid unacceptably high inflation, but not so much as to cause a recession. Managing a soft landing requires both luck and skill. Despite his maestro reputation, Greenspan had allowed the overall economy, the housing market, and the credit markets to run too hot in his final two years as chair. He intended his slow, deliberate interest rate hikes in 2004 and 2005 to avoid shocking the economy, but he failed to impose enough restraint. As a result, Bernanke inherited bubbles in the housing and credit markets and an incipient inflation problem. In other words, he climbed into the pilot's seat as the plane was overshooting the runway.

As Bernanke took control, the weather changed. As a Fed governor, Bernanke argued that 1 to 2 percent was an acceptable range for his preferred measure of inflation—the *core personal consumption deflator*, a measure of consumer prices that excludes the volatile food and energy components.[7] Core inflation had been inside the 1-to-2 percent "Bernanke boundaries" when Greenspan retired, but now—just a few months into the new chair's term, the data had been revised upward to show inflation running above the Bernanke boundaries (figure 1-2). So much for the soft landing.

FIGURE 1-2

Core PCE inflation

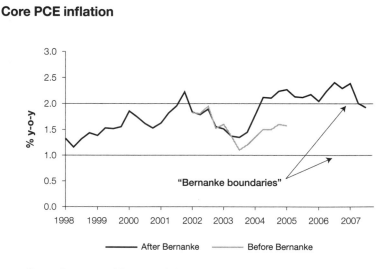

Even in the best of times, Bernanke would have faced a tough balancing act. On the one hand, he wanted to demonstrate continuity with the previous Fed chair. Certainly there was much to learn from his legendary predecessor both as an economist and as a policy maker. Moreover, after Greenspan's success, the public wasn't looking for change. During the 2000 campaign, Republican presidential candidate John McCain joked that if Greenspan were to expire during a McCain presidency, he would put sunglasses on the corpse and prop it up in a chair, as in the movie *Weekend at Bernie's*.[8] On the other hand, Bernanke needed to establish his own identity. Ben Bernanke and Alan Greenspan share many views about the way the Fed should act, but there are important differences as well. This question brings us to the subject of this book.

WHO IS BEN BERNANKE?

For most Americans, Alan Greenspan *was* the Fed. So how does Bernanke differ from Greenspan? To understand the answer to this question, you need to understand how Bernanke fits in to the evolving art of central banking.

Economists are famous for having two answers to every question, but a consensus has emerged on how central banks should frame, analyze, and communicate policy. The analytical framework is a synthesis of the two main strains of macroeconomics: the classical and Keynesian schools (discussed in detail in chapter 2). Smaller outposts for other approaches still thrive, but just as English has become the dominant international language, the Classical-Keynesian synthesis frames the monetary policy debate. Bernanke is an important contributor to the synthesis framework, whose proponents argue that a central bank can help steer the economy away from recessions, but if it oversteers and cases too much, serious inflation problems can emerge.

The methodological approach is also a synthesis. Thirty years ago, many economists hoped that complex computer models of the economy could turn macroeconomic forecasting into a precise science. Today, most economists understand that the world changes too fast and is too complex for models alone to be effective predictors. Bernanke is a member of this new generation of central bankers.

Economists at the Fed and other central banks combine three approaches: big multi-equation models developed with the latest in high-tech statistics; smaller, more flexible single-sector models; and the data trend analysis familiar to business economists like myself. When Bernanke assumed the Fed chair, skeptics argued that Greenspan had been a master at data analysis, while Bernanke is too much of a model-based academic to make policy effectively. However, in his years as a Fed governor Bernanke "double majored" in the art and science of economic forecasting. Indeed, his approach may well prove a better mix than Greenspan's lobsterlike grasp of data trends.

Perhaps the biggest change for the new generation is communication. In Greenspan's generation, a constant barrage of political pressure put central bankers on the defensive, encouraging purposeful obscurity. Paul Volcker, a devoted cigar-smoker and Fed chair from 1979 to 1987, would literally and figuratively blow smoke at congressional hearings, baffling congressmen with complex economic arguments. Greenspan continued this tradition with "Fedspeak"—speeches with hidden code words that only experienced Fed watchers could understand. Only with great reluctance did Greenspan become more open during the second half of his term. By contrast, Bernanke's generation of policy makers believes strongly in transparency—that central bankers should clearly present their economic views and the likely policy path.

BEND IT LIKE BERNANKE: HOW
BERNANKE WILL SHAPE THE FED

Which framework does the Fed under Bernanke use to analyze the economy? How does the Fed's rather Byzantine decision process work? Why does moving a tiny lever like the federal funds rate, the borrowing rate between banks, have such enormous effects on the economy and capital markets? How does the Fed interact with politicians and the public? This book tackles these questions as follows.

In chapter 2, "How the World Works," I lay out how the Fed fits into the broader economic and financial market environment. Even to investment professionals, macroeconomics can seem like a bewildering array of competing models. But, in the economic and policy debate at the Fed, a relatively simple framework tends to dominate discussion. Fear not: you don't need six years of college and ten years of graduate school to get the basic argument. I'll present this consensus framework and Bernanke's contributions to it quickly and painlessly.

In chapter 3, "Secrets of the Temple," I describe how the Fed manages the economy. The Fed's principle policy lever is changing the federal funds rate. The funds rate is not directly important to the economy, but changes in the funds rate set off a chain of effects through almost the whole capital market—stocks, bonds, and exchange rates all react when the Fed moves the funds rate. Bernanke is an important contributor to understanding this monetary policy transmission mechanism. Indeed, to understand how the Fed will respond to the ongoing crisis in credit markets, you must understand his work on the role of credit markets in the economy.

In chapter 4, "Declaration of Independence," and chapter 5, "Blowing Smoke," I look at how the Fed interacts with politicians and the public. I argue that, as with the Supreme Court, there is a good reason to keep monetary policy independent of the political process. Fortunately, today the Fed is as strong and independent as it has ever been. Increased independence has gone hand in hand with more transparency—more clear communication with the public. It is important that investors stop looking for hidden messages from the Fed. Bernanke should be taken much more at his word than Greenspan.

I then turn to Bernanke's benchmark, Greenspan himself. By the time Greenspan retired, the words *Greenspan* and *the Fed* were interchangeable. Thus it is difficult to analyze Bernanke without having some perspective on his larger-than-life predecessor. Popular perceptions of Greenspan seem to gravitate to two extremes:

either he is a superhuman character with remarkable economic and policy skills or he is the guy who created "serial bubbles" in the stock and credit markets and who compromised the Fed by endorsing the Bush tax cut. Chapter 6 discusses his successes and chapter 7 presents the downside of his chairmanship. Greenspan surely deserves credit for the strong performance of the economy during his chairmanship, but he also had some notable mistakes, including thrusting himself unnecessarily into political matters and failing to respond to bubbles in asset markets.

Bernanke brings a fairly ambitious agenda to the Fed. He wants to complete the war on inflation by dictating, on paper, unconditional surrender. This insistence on a formal inflation goal does not mean he is an "inflation nutter"—someone who believes in achieving a rigid target at all costs. Rather he recognizes that the Fed has a dual mandate: to maintain maximum employment as well as price stability. In adopting a target, the Fed would simply be following current views of best practices in central banking. Chapter 8, "Constrained Discretion," presents the logic and prospects for a formal inflation target.

Bernanke is a close student of both the Great Depression and Japan's "lost decade" of economic malaise in the 1990s. In chapter 9, I explain how Bernanke's "Depression Obsession" has, and will, color his policy choices, including the decision to adopt unusually aggressive policy easing when deflation or financial market collapse threatens.

There are notable changes in style as well as substance under Bernanke. The internal workings of the Fed are changing. Over time, Greenspan became increasingly dominant over his committee. At key decision points, his view seemingly held sway. He also seemed increasingly willing to make his own calls on the economy, relying more on pragmatic business economics tools and "gut instincts" and less on staff views and models. For those of us Fed watchers, guessing the Fed's next move increasingly involved assessing Greenspan's view rather than weighing the views of the committee. Chapter 10, "Glasnost," describes Bernanke's more democratic Fed, which relies more on the traditional economics toolkit and a diversity of voices. Effective Fed watching requires sorting through these voices.

The consensus on how central banks should communicate changed during Greenspan's term and he reluctantly conceded ground. Bernanke will continue that process, and so investors should throw out their "Greenspan decoder ring" and get used to a plain speaking Fed. In chapter 11, "Zen and the Art of Monetary Maintenance," I discuss changes in how the Fed communicates to the public. This new communication style has confused the markets at times: this chapter should help readers avoid that confusion.

Perhaps the most controversial question in central banking is, "How should the Fed react to booms and busts in asset markets?" Both Bernanke and Greenspan believe that central banks simply cannot identify and manage market bubbles. If the housing or the stock markets heat up, then the Fed should address the simulative effects of rising asset prices on the economy (e.g., if people feel wealthier, they spend more), not the risk of a bubble. If and when the bubble pops, the Fed should aggressively counter any economic impact. In chapter 12, "See No Evil, Hear No Evil, Speak No Evil," I describe the logic behind this asymmetric approach to bubble management and I explain why I disagree with the Fed, favoring a lean-against-the-bubble policy when asset bubbles are suspected.

Chapter 13, "Radical Risk Management," explains why the Bernanke Fed seemed to suddenly shift gears in 2008 and adopted a very aggressive approach to supporting the capital markets and the economy. I argue that Bernanke's actions come right out of his study of the Great Depression, Japan's deflation, and the role of credit markets in the economy. Understanding his background is crucial to predicting how the Fed will respond to future stress in the economy and markets.

MIDTERM GRADE

After only a couple years at the helm, it is much too early to pass final judgment on the Bernanke Fed. I am in the business of forecasting and guiding investment decisions—I'm not a historian. Chapter 14, "Murphy's Law," and chapter 15, "Pressure Cooker," look at the incredibly challenging policy environment Bernanke inherited from Greenspan and attempt to give him a midterm grade. The Bernanke Fed has been pillared from all sides: some argue it eased policy too much, rewarding risk takers and igniting inflation; others say it has eased policy too little, risking a financial and economic meltdown. In reality, I believe the Bernanke Fed has done a reasonable job with the hand it has been dealt.

What is the outlook for the Bernanke Fed? I would expect a continued aggressive response to likely further economic weakness. I also think the Fed has learned two lessons from the housing bubble: lean against signs of an emerging bubble and don't wait too long to normalize interest rates once the economy finds its feet.

As this book goes to press, a hot topic on the weekend business shows is whether Bernanke should or could be replaced at the end of his four-year term in 2010. I believe it would be a serious blow to the institution to replace a rapidly learning expert on monetary policy with either a "practical" businessperson or a political appointee. Bill Clinton's and George W. Bush's hands-off approach to the Fed has served the economy and financial markets well. We should judge the Bernanke Fed relative to what it inherited: a nasty cocktail of popping asset bubbles and building inflation pressures. The Bernanke-led Fed has had communication problems and its share of rookie mistakes. However, in terms of policy actions, I doubt even his legendary predecessor would have done any better.

PART I

BERNANKE'S BACKDROP

The Federal Reserve's Role
in the Economy

Before we zero in on Bernanke and his benchmark, Alan Greenspan, we must understand the Fed's role in the economy. After more than twenty years as a Fed economist and as a Fed watcher, I am still amazed by the misconceptions and mythology that surround the Fed. As I will show, the Fed has a Byzantine decision-making process, but the veil can be cut through quite easily. The Fed is not an omnipotent manager of the economy, but is more like a tugboat steering an oil tanker in rough waters. Other than getting data releases a day or two early and access to some anecdotal information, the Fed does not have

11

some inside scoop on the economy that mere mortal business econo-
mists do not have—I did not become less well informed when I left the
Fed for the Street in 1996. Moreover, the Fed really has only one tool
for managing the economy—changing the funds rate—hence it can-
not fight inflation, stimulate growth, and manage capital markets all
at the same time. It must pick its battles.

I will also look at how the Fed interacts with the public and politi-
cians. There are good reasons to keep the Fed independent of the politi-
cal process—monetary policy is best left to "econocrats" worried about
their legacy in history, not politicians worried about the next election.
Fortunately, today the Fed is as strong and independent as it has ever
been. Increased independence has gone hand in hand with more trans-
parency in the way the Fed communicates with the public. Trans-
parency and independence are self-reinforcing: if the Fed is left to do its
job, then it should communicate more clearly about what it is doing; if
the Fed is clearer about its actions, then the public will trust it more.

2

How the World Works

A Brief Course in Macroeconomics

Getting into the head of the Fed requires a basic primer on how the economy and monetary policy works. Macroeconomics is often presented as a bewildering array of competing models, and certainly there is plenty of disagreement within the profession. Nonetheless, a relatively simple framework underlies much of the discussion at central banks today. Central to this framework is the relationship between growth and inflation.

THE BULWARK

Central banking essentially involves a trade-off between promoting low and stable inflation and low and stable unemployment. By law, the Federal Reserve has an explicit dual mandate, where unemployment and inflation are given equal weight (for some other central banks the inflation objective is dominant). When financial crises emerge, central banks typically downplay these two concerns and focus on maintaining the integrity of the financial system.

Why worry about *both* unemployment and inflation? The cost of high unemployment is obvious; less obvious is the cost of inflation. In their introductory textbook, Robert Frank and Ben Bernanke list five costs of inflation:[1]

- *Noise in the price system:* "When inflation is high . . . the subtle signals that are transmitted through the price system become more difficult to interpret," hurting economic efficiency.

- *Distortions to the tax system:* Indexing the whole tax system to inflation is difficult; and so, as inflation rises, it can change the after-tax return to different activities, distorting the economy.

- *"Shoe-leather costs":* When inflation and interest rates are high people will try to keep their cash balances low and will end up spending a lot of effort conserving cash.

- *Unexpected redistribution of wealth:* An unexpected surge in inflation hurts people on fixed income and redistributes wealth from savers to borrowers. The uncertainty undercuts savings.

- *Interference with long-run planning:* Inflation makes it harder to plan future costs and returns for companies and households.

Interestingly, studies that try to estimate the cost of inflation find significant effects when inflation is very high, but give no clear guidance on how low is low enough. Moreover, as I will discuss in more detail later, inflation can be too low as well as too high, particularly if inflation turns into deflation—that is, if there is a steady fall in prices. Nonetheless, many central banks today have inflation targets designed to keep inflation low and avoid the slippery slope of allowing a small inflation pick-up to turn into a large inflation pick-up.

THE SYNTHESIS

The current consensus approach to central banking emerged from the two major economic disasters of the last century—the Great Depression of the 1930s and the Great Inflation of the 1970s.[2] These respective periods of mass unemployment and mass inflation across the developed world sparked a massive economics literature. The Depression spawned *Keynesian* economics: models of how frictions in the economy prevent smooth adjustments to shocks. In a Keynesian world, if unemployment were high, policy makers could push it back down through tax cuts, spending increases, or lowering interest of rates. Similarly, if inflation were too high, policy makers could push it back down by raising interest rates, cutting spending, or raising taxes.

By the 1960s there was growing confidence among many macroeconomists that policy makers could fine-tune the economy in the same way that psychologists hoped to tame mental disorder. The Great Inflation of the 1970s, with consumer prices surging across the industrial world, undercut this confidence. This spawned a revival of *classical* economics: the view that attempts to stimulate the economy beyond its productive limits could lead to an ever rising spiral of inflation.

The synthesis was to accept elements of both theories. Keynesians had it right in the short run, recognizing the need to push the economy back on course when unemployment or inflation became too high. New Classicalists had it right in the long run: pushing too hard for too long generated out-of-control inflation. Both sides of this debate tried to claim the center ground: the resulting fusion was called *New Keynesian* by some and the *New Neo-Classical Synthesis* by others. To the outsider this looks a bit like trying to distinguish a Compassionate Conservative from a New Democrat.

Because it draws on the two main branches of macroeconomics, one of the virtues of the synthesis is its flexibility. Most central bankers are neither pure Keynesians nor pure classicalists, but somewhere in between. Hence most central bankers—including

Greenspan and Bernanke—accept the synthesis as the main framework for policy discussion.

Central to the synthesis is a simple model of the relationship between economic growth and price inflation (figure 2-1). The conventional model of inflation can be described as a set of traffic laws for noninflationary growth. *Potential output growth* is the limit on how fast the economy can grow without driving the unemployment rate down: when the economy grows at its potential or trend rate, employment tends to rise at the same rate as new workers entering the job market, leaving the unemployment rate constant. If growth is above potential, the unemployment rate falls. Potential growth is determined by longer term economic forces such as the growth in the working age population and the rate of technological advance. Over the years potential growth has varied, but currently most economists believe the U.S. economy can grow at between 2.5 and 3 percent without putting downward pressure on the unemployment rate.

Okun's Law shows how quickly the unemployment rate falls if GDP growth exceeds potential. In recent decades, the unemployment rate has tended to fall by about 0.4 percentage points if GDP growth is a percentage point above potential for a year. Thus if the unemployment rate were say 6 percent at the start of the year and GDP grows one percentage point above potential, then typically the unemployment rate would fall to 5.6 percent by the start of the next year.

The second traffic law for inflation is the *nonaccelerating inflation rate of unemployment* (NAIRU). This is the limit on how far the unemployment rate can fall before inflation picks up. When the unemployment rate gets too low there is a scramble for workers,

FIGURE 2-1

The traffic laws of inflation

driving up wages and putting pressure on prices. Moreover, when unemployment is low, other resources are usually also in tight supply, adding to inflation pressures. The *Phillips Curve* (described in detail below) shows how much inflation rises if the unemployment rate falls below NAIRU.

The easiest way to understand this model is to consider what happens during a typical period of economic recovery from recession. Normally, growth is strong in the early part of the recovery, with GDP growing faster than the potential, or trend growth rate. This rapid growth puts downward pressure on the unemployment rate. However, inflation usually falls in this initial stage of rapid growth because there is still slack or excess unemployment in the economy. Only after an extended period of strong growth does the unemployment rate fall enough to reach NAIRU and trigger a rise in inflation.

A popular mantra of conservative commentators is that growth does not cause inflation. Indeed, as I noted above, inflation often falls in the early parts of business expansions despite strong growth. Moreover, strong growth can go on indefinitely without causing inflation if the economy has a high potential rate of growth—that is, a natural tendency to grow rapidly, owing to strong technological innovation or population growth. However, in the synthesis model *excessive* growth is inflationary: if growth is strong enough for long enough to create a low enough unemployment rate and other signs of tight capacity, then growth ultimately does lead to inflation.

NAIRUVANA

The most important part of this framework is the *Phillips Curve*—the relationship between unemployment and inflation (figure 2-2). Indeed, if readers learn nothing else from this book, they should understand the modern Phillips Curve. In 1958 the New Zealand economist Bill Phillips discovered that inflation tended to be low during periods of high unemployment and inflation tended to be high when unemployment was low.[3]

FIGURE 2-2

The original Phillips Curve

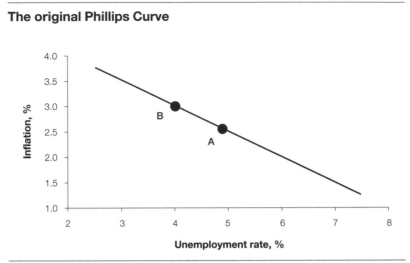

Unemployment rate, %

The logic is simple: when unemployment is high, competition among workers desperate for jobs will put downward pressure on wages. Since wages are the most important component of business costs—around 70 percent on average—this will put downward pressure on prices. Moreover, periods of high unemployment generally suggest broader economic weakness and a lack of pricing power for companies. For many years, central bankers believed they could choose points along this curve—if you want low inflation and are willing to tolerate some unemployment, choose point A; if you want lower unemployment then you would have to accept higher inflation (point B). This is in fact not right; but as I will show later, the original Phillips Curve continues to underpin populist views of how the economy works.

However, in the late 1960s not one, but two, future Noble Prize winners—Ned Phelps and Milton Friedman—argued that the Phillips Curve is not stable.[4] They argued that if the unemployment rate is pushed below its natural, or NAIRU, threshold, then inflation will initially rise mildly as the original Phillips Curve assumed. But that is not the end of the story; once firms and workers recognize the higher inflation, they will seek to pad their wage and price increases with a general inflation adjustment. In terms of the diagram, the Phillips Curve will shift up, and the new combination of unemployment and inflation would be much higher (point C on figure 2-3). Ouch. It gets worse. Attempting to keep the unemployment rate permanently below the natural rate will set up a spiral of wage and price increases. Over time, contracts will be designed to include automatic adjustments for rising costs, making the spiral even tougher. In other words, holding the unemployment rate too low for too long will cause a replay of the Great Inflation of the 1970s.

Of course, in practice, figuring out the NAIRU is very difficult. At any given moment, some people will naturally be between jobs. This reflects matching problems: workers may need to relocate due to a declining industry, they may have out-of-date skills, they may be looking for an ideal position, and so forth. In a dynamic economy, there are always pockets of high unemployment resulting from the rise and fall of industries and regions. Milton Friedman thought it was so hard to pin down the NAIRU, it probably was not practically useful as a tool for predicting inflation and setting monetary

FIGURE 2-3

The modern Phillips Curve

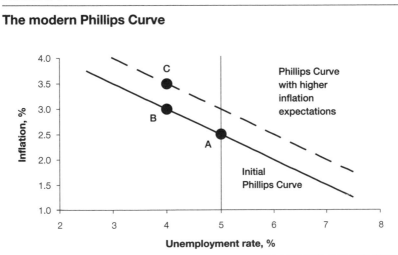

policy. But the current consensus is that the modern Phillips Curve is a rough, but key, gauge to policy.

Most economists think the NAIRU is lower today (about 5 percent) than it was in the 1970s and 1980s (6 percent or higher). Job matching is easier with the use of the Internet. As the baby boom generation ages there has been an increase in the number of middle-aged workers with strong motivation to minimize gaps between jobs, and there has been a drop in the share of high-unemployment teenagers in the job market. The decline in union power and a relatively low minimum wage probably have also contributed to a lower NAIRU—both tend to keep wages artificially high, contributing to unemployment. Perhaps the most esoteric factor lowering NAIRU is the rising prison population: these often hard-to-employ people drop out of the statistics when they are incarcerated. When the unemployment rate dipped below the 5 percent NAIRU level in 2006, concerns about inflation emerged (figure 2-4).

FIGURE 2-4

The unemployment threshold for inflation

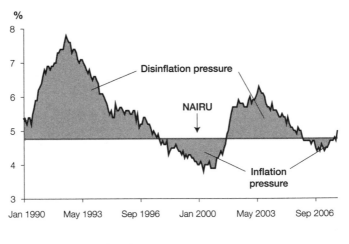

Source: Bureau of Labor Statistics.

WEALTH (EFFECT) IS NOT EVERYTHING

When it became clear that Ben Bernanke was the heir apparent to the Fed chairmanship, one of the first things I did was to buy Bernanke's intermediate textbook *Macroeconomics*, coauthored with Andrew B. Abel.[5] Why would someone with a PhD buy an undergraduate text? I reasoned that this would give me a quick way to judge Bernanke's view on any issue that he had not spoken about as a Fed official.

Bernanke's writings and speeches both suggest his views are generally well within the macroeconomics consensus. One key area of departure is his work on the interactions between credit markets, the economy, and monetary policy. Bernanke is a proponent of the *financial accelerator model*: the idea that strong financial and credit conditions and a strong economy can reinforce each other to create economic booms (and that weak conditions can interact to create busts). During booms, both firms and households have stronger incomes and their assets are worth more, encouraging relaxed lending rules. Easy lending makes the economy even stronger and that, in turn, encourages even easier lending standards. Bernanke also believes credit conditions can influence how effective the Fed is in managing the economy. Disruptions to capital markets in 2007 have brought this seemingly dry academic topic back to life.[6]

Quantifying these credit channels is very difficult, so most formal statistical models of the economy ignore the details of the financial sector. However, work by Nobel Prize winners George Akerlof and Joseph Stiglitz showed that frictions in the credit markets are important in understanding the linkages between financial markets and the real economy. Examples of such frictions include imperfect information about the true risk characteristics of borrowers and the cost of monitoring borrowers. These frictions cause the lender to charge a higher interest rate for loans. In the jargon of economics there is an *external finance premium*—a spread of borrowing over the cost of self-financing. Since credit is the grease of economic growth, these frictions are important to forecasting the economy.

THE FINANCIAL ACCELERATOR
AND THE MORTGAGE MESS

Bernanke's research came in handy when the credit crisis kicked in starting in 2007. While the financial accelerator literature concentrates mainly on the corporate sector, it can be applied to households as well. The literature offers a richer means of exploring the interactions between home prices, interest rates, credit standards, real estate lending, and economic growth.

In the traditional model, a strong housing market stimulates the economy through two channels: increased construction and increased consumer spending via the *wealth effect*. Specifically, as home values rise and consumers feel wealthier, they choose to spend more. They can finance this spending by borrowing against their homes, borrowing through other arrangements, or simply putting less money aside for savings. Estimates of the wealth effect vary widely, but at Lehman Brothers we assume that as home values rise and the increases are seen as permanent, homeowners raise their consumption by six cents for every dollar of additional wealth. For example, if the value of a home jumps by $100,000, the typical household will ratchet up annual consumption by $6,000 and keep it there. That would imply that the whole windfall of wealth is spent in just seventeen years—not a very responsible financial plan!

Bernanke and other advocates of the financial accelerator model argue that the wealth effect may not capture the full impact of the housing boom. When home values rise, consumers have more collateral against which to borrow. This is particularly true with the rapid innovations in the mortgage business and sharp decline in transaction costs for mortgage loans. Thus during the boom, increasing collateral values and easing lending standards may have accelerated the impact on consumer spending on the way up; and during the recent bust, the opposite may be happening (figure 2-5). Frederic Mishkin, Bernanke's past coauthor and current colleague at the Fed, has laid out these potential add-on effects in

FIGURE 2-5

Home price inflation

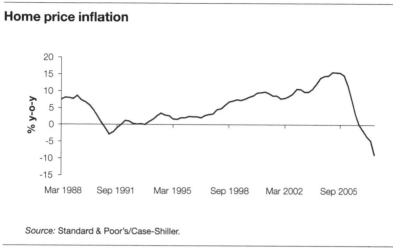

several recent speeches.[7] This thinking probably played a major role in the Fed's decision to ease policy aggressively in the fall of 2007, before clear signs of broad economic weakness emerged.

As Bernanke himself has acknowledged, "Although the financial accelerator seems intuitive—certainly financial and credit conditions tend to be pro-cyclical—nailing down this mechanism empirically has not proven entirely straight forward."[8] Researchers in the United Kingdom have found that rising interest rates tend to have a bigger impact on consumer spending when imperfections exist in the credit market.[9] The scale of the effect is large—particularly for home building and home prices.

The financial accelerator literature implies that economists and investors should focus on a broad range of financial indicators. Normally, investors can get a good sense of how capital markets are doing by tracking core parts of the capital market—Treasury interest rates, stock market indexes such as the S&P 500, and the exchange rate of the dollar versus major currencies such as the Euro. However, during credit crises economists keep a close eye on several measures of financial distress.

For banks, the best indicator of stress is the Fed's latest Senior Lending Officer's Survey: on a quarterly basis the Fed asks banks about their lending policies. Surveys in the summer and fall of 2007 showed tighter lending standards spreading from one sector to another. It started in the mortgage market: about a third of mortgage loans that were made in the prior two years were no longer being made under the new tighter credit standards. The Fed's survey and other data showed the pull-back in credit gradually spread to jumbo mortgages and finally to virtually every class of loans (figure 2-6).

For credit markets, the best indicator of stress is the interest rate spread—the extra interest charged for a loan to a risky borrower relative to the rate for a safe borrower (like the U.S. government). This differential gives a sense of the level of confidence in the economy and the extra borrowing costs being imposed on firms and individuals. In academic work, the spread most often examined is the spread between commercial paper (a source of short-term funds for corporations) and Treasury bills. However, a variety of other spreads are a useful gauge of stress, including the spreads on

FIGURE 2-6

Net percent of banks reporting tighter lending standards

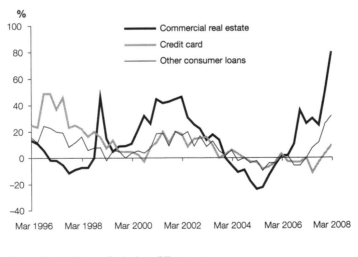

Source: Federal Reserve Senior Loan Officer survey.

high-grade and junk bonds from corporations. These spreads widened sharply in the recent financial crisis, a strong signal to the Bernanke Fed that the economy was at risk.

WIDE AWAKE—AND SANE

Ben Bernanke is often portrayed as too academic to handle the real-world challenges of monetary policy. As turmoil in the money and credit markets intensified in August 2007, CNBC reporter Jim Cramer blasted away at Bernanke, repeating over and over: "Bernanke is being an academic, he has no idea how bad it is out there, no idea . . . he's nuts, they're nuts, they know nothing . . . the Fed is asleep."[10]

Cramer must have been talking about another Ben Bernanke, because nothing could be further from the truth. How could one of the leading experts on the financial accelerator model be oblivious to developments in the credit markets? The Open Market Desk at the Federal Reserve Bank of New York always keeps a finger on the pulse of financial markets; during the 2007 credit crunch, Fed officials in and out of New York were particularly active, talking to market participants ranging from the executive suite to the traders in the trenches. Records released under the Freedom of Information Act show that in 2007 Bernanke himself met with a diverse group: financial and business executives, leading politicians, academic experts, foreign central bankers, Treasury officials, and a certain well-known former Fed chairman (need I mention Greenspan's name?).[11]

In my nine years at the Federal Reserve Bank of New York I was fully indoctrinated into the synthesis view. Moreover, people like myself are heavily represented among business economists, with a particularly high concentration on Wall Street. The synthesis view fits very well with the natural instincts of a central banker. The Keynesian side of the view leaves a role for active monetary policy—why work for the Fed if you do not believe monetary policy has a role in stabilizing the economy? The classical side of the view shows why the central bank needs to be an independent guardian against inflation. The flexible nature of the model accommodates diverse arguments. Bernanke, as an important proponent of the synthesis model during his academic career at Stanford and Princeton, is well equipped to deal with today's economic challenges.

3

Secrets of the Temple

Demystifying the Fed

In William Greider's famous book, *The Secrets of the Temple*, the Fed is described as a mysterious—almost religious—institution: "The governors of the Federal Reserve decided the largest of questions of the political economy, including who shall prosper and who shall fail, yet their role remained opaque and mysterious."[1] While this was partly true when the book was published in 1987, today there are no secrets, and the core principals can be explained in a few pages. So let's take a look at how the Fed manages the economy. Let's explore the Fed's complicated decision structure, how changes in the interest rates the Fed controls work their way into the economy, how uncertainty affects policy choices, and how the Fed deals with the toughest policy challenge: supply shocks—a disruption to the economy, such as a surge in oil prices, that both weakens growth and raises inflation.

PAY CLOSE ATTENTION TO THAT MAN
BEHIND THE CURTAIN

The Fed has a remarkably arcane decision process, a leftover of the Federal Reserve Act of 1913—the original legislation that called it into being—and the amended legislation in the 1930s. The main policy-making group is the Federal Open Market Committee (FOMC), which comprises the presidents of the twelve regional Federal Reserve banks and the seven governors (including Bernanke) who reside in Washington, D.C. However, at any given meeting only twelve members vote—all seven governors, the president of the Federal Reserve Bank of New York, and four Reserve Bank presidents. These four voting slots rotate annually among the remaining eleven banks. The FOMC has eight scheduled meetings annually, rather oddly spaced across the year in five- to eight-week intervals. (Here's my unsolicited advice to the Fed: why doesn't it meet on a monthly basis like most other central banks?)

While in theory the Fed chairman is just one among equals, in practice the position can be quite powerful. The large size of the FOMC can get in the way of efficient decision making. Moving the discussion forward and taking timely actions requires effective leadership. Indeed, I would argue that as long as the chair has the respect of the committee, the large size of the group enhances his power.[2] The Fed chair controls the agenda and the flow of discussion at meetings and frames the choices at the end of each meeting. Members are reluctant to speak out aggressively against the chairman's policy choices for fear of undercutting the institution. More broadly, the chairman benefits from his role as the public face of the Fed.

Stepping back, the whole thing is a bit like the seemingly arbitrary old British system of measurement—20 pence in a shilling and 12 shillings in a pound; 12 inches in a foot and 3 feet in a yard; and so on. Some of the elaborate rules are a deliberate attempt to put checks and balances into the system, but some of the structure reflects the political reality around the founding of the Fed. For example, two out of the twelve Federal Reserve Banks are in Missouri because James A. Reed, the powerful Democratic senator from that state at the time the banks were founded, insisted on it. The Fed has strongly resisted legislation to change its bizarre structure because it fears that any new law could include changes that hurt its independence. And because its processes are so complicated, it's natural that books like *The Secrets of the Temple* should be written.

ARCHIMEDES' LEVER

One of the remarkable things about Fed policy is that its seemingly small policy levers can have a transformative impact on financial markets and the economy. The main policy tool is the federal funds rate—the borrowing rate between commercial banks. At any given time, some banks have extra reserves and some have a shortage of reserves. In the funds market, banks with excess reserves lend to those that are short-handed. The Fed controls the funds rate by buying and selling bonds to banks: When it sells bonds, it pulls reserves out of the banks, thus putting upward pressure on the funds rate as banks scramble for liquidity; when it buys bonds, it creates downward pressure on the funds rate.

The Fed's second, less important, policy tool is the discount rate—the rate the Fed charges when it lends directly to banks. In this case, the interest rate is set by the seven governors, rather than the full FOMC. In practice, even though only a subset of the FOMC sets the discount rate, the two interest rates are moved up and down in a coordinated fashion.[3]

Changing the funds rate is just the beginning of how the Fed impacts the economy. Indeed, a popular misconception is that the *tightness* (when the funds rate is raised) or *ease* (when the funds rate is lowered) of monetary policy can be judged by simply looking at the funds rate. For example, when the Fed was hiking rates between the summer of 2004 and the summer of 2006, a lot of ink was spilled in deciding what the Fed's *neutral* (i.e., the rate at which the Fed was neither stimulating nor depressing the economy) rate was. As figure 3-1 shows, over the last fifty years the "real

FIGURE 3-1

The nominal and "real" funds rate

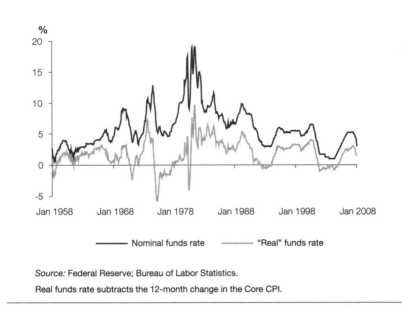

Source: Federal Reserve; Bureau of Labor Statistics.
Real funds rate subtracts the 12-month change in the Core CPI.

funds rate"—that is, the difference between the funds rate and consumer price inflation—has averaged about 2 percentage points.
Hence, when the funds rate reached 4.5 percent—or about 2 percentage points above inflation—at the start of 2006, a number of
Fed officials argued that the funds rate was in the neighborhood of
neutral. When asked what the neutral rate was in Congressional testimony, however, then-Chairman Alan Greenspan ducked the question by saying the neutral funds rate was a moving target and that
"we probably will know it when we are there."[4]

NATTERING NABOBS OF NEUTRALITY

In reality, there is a good reason to duck this question: judging the
tightness of policy is too complicated to summarize in one number.
As Abel and Bernanke argue in their textbook, *Macroeconomics*,
"judgment about whether monetary policy is expansionary or con-
tractionary depends on the relative strength of the different [policy]

channels."[5] The funds and discount rate are not directly important to the economy. Assessing the strength of monetary policy requires weighing the complex transmission from the funds rate, through financial markets and to the economy.

When the Fed raises or lowers the funds rate, it sets off a chain reaction through the capital markets. For a tightening, this monetary transmission mechanism involves three major channels:

1. Higher interest rates for business and consumer borrowers discourages spending.

2. The dollar exchange rate tends to rise, making U.S. products more expensive relative to foreign products and shifting spending away from the United States.

3. The stock and housing markets weaken, causing a negative wealth effect on consumer spending.

Bernanke and other advocates of the financial accelerator effect point to a fourth policy channel—the credit channel. When the Fed tightens monetary policy, the value of homes and stocks is lowered, meaning there is less collateral for loans. Tighter policy also weakens the outlook for income and profit growth. Recognizing the weakened balance sheets, financial markets apply tougher standards to some borrowers (e.g., requiring higher collateralization or simply charging higher interest rates). Bernanke believes that it is hard to understand the power of monetary policy unless proper account is taken of the interaction between policy, the economy, and credit markets.

Many economists have tried to distill financial conditions into a single index. However, most of these indexes manage to capture only a few key elements of the monetary transmission mechanism. For example, they will look at an average of market interest rates, rather than just the funds rate, and they will incorporate the impact of the exchange rate. In reality the economy is too complex and the nature of shocks to financial markets changes too much to consistently summarize financial conditions with one number. Reading these tea leaves is complicated. In this respect there really are some secrets to the temple.

NO PAIN, NO GAIN

Understanding these channels is central to explaining Bernanke's policy decisions during his first two years as Fed chairman. When Bernanke replaced Greenspan, the mantra on Wall Street was "one and done," meaning that after fourteen rate hikes in a row under Greenspan, the Bernanke Fed would hike rates just one more time. Instead, the FOMC extended the tightening streak to seventeen meetings in a row. Then after keeping the funds rate unchanged for more than a year, in the fall of 2007 the Bernanke Fed abruptly cut the funds rate by 100 basis points over three meetings. At the time of this writing, the Fed had cut another 200 basis points in the first quarter of 2008, with hints of further cuts to come.

Table 3-1 shows how some of the policy channels have operated over this period. For most of the June 2004 to June 2006 rate hike cycle, capital markets largely ignored the Fed. In a normal tightening cycle, a 350-basis-point rise in the funds rate would have raised ten-year yields by 100 to 200 basis points; however, in this cycle, ten-year yields remained unchanged. Moreover, credit spreads fell to record lows, banks eased rather than tightened lending standards, the stock market steadily rallied, the dollar was essentially flat, and home price inflation accelerated. No wonder the Fed kept raising rates: not only was it not imposing any restraint, financial conditions were easing as the Fed tightened.

All this changed in 2006, when the housing market finally cracked. Home buyers had been ignoring warnings of a bubble and ignoring the Fed's steady rate hikes. But finally in the fall of 2005 confidence in housing started to cool. This caused first a sharp drop in home construction and then, with a long lag, a steady slowing in home price inflation. This signaled that one of the key channels of monetary policy was working, and the Bernanke-led Fed responded by stopping the long tightening cycle. Of course, that was not the end of matters. In 2007, prompted by signs of serious problems in the mortgage market, there was a dramatic "risk-aversion trade" in the capital markets. By the fall of 2007, financial conditions were not only no longer easy, they were tight. A funds

TABLE 3-1

Key measures of financial conditions

	Start of rate hikes	End of Greenspan	Bernanke era	
	Jun-04	Dec-05	Dec-06	Dec-07
Fed funds rate (%)	1.00	4.50	5.25	4.00
Ten-year Treasury yield (%)	4.7	4.5	4.6	4.1
S&P 500 index (%y-o-y)	14.7	5.2	2.2	4.4
Trade-weighted dollar (%y-o-y)	−1.3	2.5	−4.5	−6.8
National home prices (%y-o-y)	15.6	14.7	0.2	−8.9
High-yield bond spread (bp)	389	353	291	551

Source: Federal Reserve; Department of Commerce; Standard & Poor's/Case-Shiller; Lehman Brothers.

rate of 5.25 percent made sense when the markets were in a happy mood, but not when the markets were steadily tightening. The Bernanke-led Fed quickly cut rates to offset the tightening of credit conditions (figure 3-2).

FIGURE 3-2

The federal funds rate

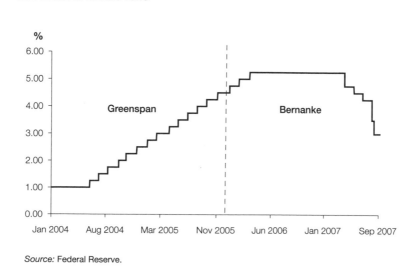

Source: Federal Reserve.

SUPPLY-SIDE ECONOMICS

Up to this point we have focused on how the Fed trades off inflation and unemployment. But the biggest challenge to central bankers
is when a supply shock forces them to face both an unemployment
and an inflation problem simultaneously. The classic example of a
supply shock is when disruptions to the oil market drive up the cost
of oil. This surge in prices creates an impossible dilemma for the Fed
because the rise in prices increases business costs and therefore
consumer price inflation, but it also diverts consumer spending
power out of the economy, hurting growth. The Fed must decide:
should it hike rates to offset inflation pressures or lower rates to offset the weakness in consumer spending?

The typical central bank response is to wait to see which problem dominates—inflation or unemployment—and then react. As a
governor, Bernanke wrote: "The Fed's response to the inflationary
effects of an increase in oil prices should depend to some extent on
the economy's staring point . . . if inflation has been near the high
end of the acceptable range, and policymakers perceive a significant risk that the inflation and inflation expectations may rise further, then stronger action, in the form of a tighter monetary policy
may well prove necessary."[6]

The Fed's response to Hurricane Katrina is a good example of
how it handles a supply shock. When Katrina devastated the Gulf
Coast in August 2005, there was a widespread perception that the
economic devastation of the storm would alter the path of Fed policy. The Fed was at the time in the process of gradually rising interest rates, and a number of economists argued that the Fed would
stop the hikes or even cut rates.

In fact, the Fed stayed on course and continued to hike rates.
Why the callous response? In part, it was because the Fed knew the
economy had bounced back quickly from prior natural disasters.
Moreover, it knew that monetary policy was not the right policy tool
to deal with the devastation—cutting interest rates would not do
much for the Gulf, but targeted aid would. But the bigger story was
that analysts were forgetting that Katrina was a supply shock: it un-

dercut growth, but it also created inflation risks. These came mainly in the form of upward pressure on energy and construction costs, but also from a diversion of tourist activity into other parts of the economy and from spending on relief efforts. Katrina created shortages, and shortages are inflationary. The Fed did not ease or even stop its rate hikes because monetary policy cannot fix a supply shock.

THE CHAIRMAN AS TUGBOAT CAPTAIN

Central bankers, and particularly Bernanke's legendary predecessor, are sometimes depicted as powerful technocrats pulling levers to micromanage the economy. In reality, even if we accept this general framework, policy operates in a very uncertain world. All of the key parameters of the framework are subject to considerable disagreement. How fast can the economy grow without creating a tight labor market? How low can the unemployment rate go before triggering inflation? How long a period of inflation will the general public tolerate before they begin to lose confidence in the Fed and factor higher general inflation into their wages and prices? Monetary policy also works through complex and changing channels. Hence, Milton Friedman's famous observation that monetary policy works with long and variable lags.

Rather than view the Fed as an omnipotent engineer, pulling levers to micromanage the economy, a better analogy is a tugboat trying to guide an oil tanker. It is easy when the waters are calm as in 2004 and 2005 when the Greenspan Fed was slowly returning the funds rate to a more normal level. But in unstable weather, even with aggressive countervailing efforts from the Fed, the economy may drift off course. In other words, successful monetary policy involves a lot of luck. Switching analogies, like a basketball coach, the Fed gets a lot more credit—and blame—than it deserves for its management of the economy.

So there you have it: the exciting secrets of the temple. The Fed's strange decision-making structure is an artifact of political compromises from many years ago. The Fed manages the economy by manipulating the funds rate, triggering a chain reaction in asset markets. Gauging whether policy is tight or easy requires more than just comparing the funds rate to inflation, it requires weighing the impact of Fed policy via asset markets. Under Bernanke, the Fed is probably more sensitive to the role of credit markets in transmitting monetary policy. Far from having mystical powers, tugboat captain Bernanke and his crew struggle to keep the ship on course when waters turn rough.

4

Declaration of Independence

The Political Economy of Central Banking

I n the populist tradition, the Fed is not only a mysterious institution, but it also has a malevolent twist, pulling its policy levers on behalf of financial firms and the rich. Greider describes the Fed as "the crucial anomaly at the very core of representative democracy."[1] This unelected group decides "who shall prosper and who shall fail." At the extreme the Fed is viewed as part of a conspiracy to control the global economy.

This is not the way most members of the economics profession view the Fed. Fed officials are not the only federal officials that are not directly elected. The Fed's governors are very much like Supreme Court judges: they are nominated by the president and confirmed by the Senate, and they can be impeached. Fed governors serve fourteen-year rather than lifetime terms, and the chairman must be reappointed every four years. The appointment of regional Fed presidents is more indirect. They are nominated by regional boards of directors and approved by the Fed's board of governors. By statute, these regional reserve bank boards must represent banking, business, and community interests.

Belief in an independent central bank is burned into the DNA of most macroeconomists. The argument is simple: low inflation is essential for a healthy economy, and only a central bank independent of political influence can ensure low inflation. Not only do most economists support central bank independence, many countries have recently adopted legislation that greatly strengthens the independence of their central bank.[2]

A strong, independent Fed is not a given. Two recent Fed chairmen—Paul Volcker and Alan Greenspan—were effective inflation fighters. However, their predecessors, Arthur Burns (1970–1978) and G. William Miller (1978–1979), allowed inflation to surge into the double digits (figure 4-1). Burns came to the Fed with impeccable credentials, but as chairman he seemed to blame surging inflation on everything except monetary policy—budget deficits, labor unions, rising commodity prices, etc. Burns also eased monetary policy in front of the 1972 presidential election. While there is no absolute proof that this was politically motivated, he had very

FIGURE 4-1

Consumer price inflation

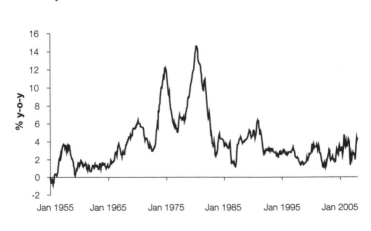

Source: Bureau of Labor Statistics.

close ties with the Nixon administration, and the episode is still viewed with some embarrassment at the Fed. G. William Miller (1978–1979) also proved unequal to the task; inflation moved higher into double digit territory during his mercifully brief eighteen-month chairmanship.

Why do so many economists favor an independent central bank? What are the evolving political pressures on the Fed? What are the prospects and pressures for Bernanke? With these questions in mind, let's take a look at the political economy of central banking.

THE CORE CONFLICT

As CSPAN addicts can attest, politicians spend a lot of time—particularly in election years—encouraging the Fed to cut interest rates; but they virtually never demand higher interest rates. This easing bias stems from the important role of the economy in elections, and from the fact that the negative impacts of easy policy—higher inflation—lag behind the positive effects—lower interest rates and stronger growth. If politicians ran the Fed, inflation would likely be a lot higher, the economy would be more unstable, and policy would tend to be particularly easy just before elections.

A number of studies have shown that the economy is the big issue when it comes to elections—particularly presidential contests. Indeed, without reference to any polls or political variables, the winners of almost every presidential election can be explained by three variables: the incumbent advantage; the negative effect of inflation; and the positive effect of strong economic growth. Figure 4-2 shows the actual vote and the predicted vote for president from a simple economic model developed by Ray Fair.[3] It is not perfect, but despite the obsession with polls and platforms, the economy is the dominant driver of election results.

Moreover, the average voter is quite shortsighted. What matters for an incumbent is not economic growth over the entire term, but in the year of the election. Here's where the lags come in. Inflation is a lagging indicator. When the Fed eases, the positive effects—stronger

FIGURE 4-2

Incumbent party vote share: Actual and predicted

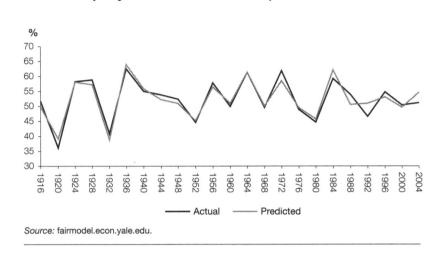

Source: fairmodel.econ.yale.edu.

growth—manifest relatively quickly, but the bad stuff—higher inflation—show up only after a long lag. Hence politicians will want the
central bank to ease policy during election years, even if it means
high inflation down the road.

Other factors add to the tension between the Fed and politicians. First, the Fed is an easy scapegoat for a poor economic backdrop. Rather than blame fiscal policy or the normal rhythms of the
business cycle, it's easy to say that it is the independent Fed—"the
crucial anomaly at the very core of representative democracy"—
that is the source of the country's economic problems.[4] The corol-
lary, perhaps (at least in the eyes of some economists), is that one
reason the Fed has retained its independence over the years is that
such independence absolves politicians from responsibility for the
tough decisions in macro policy. If politicians controlled the Fed,
who would they blame when the economy goes bad?

THE RIGHT TOOL FOR THE RIGHT JOB

An additional conflict arises from different models of how the world
works. Populist politicians do not share the consensus of macro-

economists that the Fed has no long-term impact on the unemployment rate or the distribution of income. They believe the Fed should push the unemployment rate close to zero, even at the expense of a bit more inflation, not least because low unemployment mainly benefits lower-income workers. They believe the Fed has a bias to do the opposite, keeping the unemployment rate high because low inflation helps lenders (and the rich) at the expense of borrowers (and the poor).

Economists counter that the populist view confuses short-run and long-run effects, and ignores the central role of inflation expectations. As discussed in chapter 2, the Fed cannot permanently lower the unemployment rate below its NAIRU (nonaccelerating inflation rate of unemployment), or natural, rate. There is no permanent trade-off between unemployment and inflation—if the Fed tries to hold the unemployment rate too low, it will end up with an upward spiral of inflation.

A similar argument applies to the distribution of income between lenders and borrowers. To understand why, consider the economic logic of interest rates. Lenders charge both a real interest rate (a compensation for giving up spending power temporarily) and a premium to cover expected inflation. This inflation premium compensates for inflation's lowering the purchasing power of the money when it is paid back. For example, U.S. Treasury bonds typically pay about a 3 percent real rate plus an inflation premium, so if people expect 4 percent inflation the interest rate on these bonds will be 3 percent plus 4 percent, or 7 percent. The Fed can engineer a shift of income in favor of lenders by suddenly lowering inflation—this will mean that lenders (e.g., holders of Treasury bonds) are being overcompensated for inflation. Thus if inflation is lowered to 3 percent, there is a 1 percent windfall for lenders in terms of their real spending power. However, this is almost certain to be only a temporary windfall. Once lenders and borrowers become used to the lower rate of inflation, the inflation premium will drop. Continuing the example, the new 6 percent interest rate means the old relationship between the real income of lenders and borrowers is restored.

Even if the Fed wanted to get into the income redistribution business, it simply does not have the right tools to have a meaningful impact. Moreover, attempts to engineer income redistribution would only destabilize the economy, hurting the capital markets and lowering overall income growth. If Congress wants to redistribute income, it should look to the right tool for the job—its own tax and welfare policies. Similarly, if it wants to achieve a sustained drop in the unemployment rate, Congress should implement legislation that increases incentives to work or helps match workers to jobs.

AN INDEPENDENCE ASSESSMENT

The Fed's legal structure is quite complicated, making it hard to assess its real degree of independence from political pressure. This ambiguity applies not only to the way power is shared within the system, but also in its relationship to the rest of the federal government. Statutorily, the Fed is a creature of Congress. The seven governors in Washington are appointed by the president and confirmed by the Senate. Their fourteen-year term provides considerable insulation from politics, but a governor can be impeached with a two-thirds vote of the Senate. The designation of a chairman every four years provides another potential lever of political pressure.[5] For example, Ben Bernanke's first four-year term ends in 2010, which will give the next U.S. president an opportunity to nominate a new chairman.

The regional Fed presidents are several steps removed from Washington politics. They are nominated by a local board of directors and then approved by the board of governors. These Fed officials are independent both by virtue of where they are located—spread across the country in twelve separate reserve banks—and by the appointment (and firing) process. It should not be a surprise that the regional presidents have historically been more likely to dissent at Federal Open Market Committee (FOMC) meetings and have tended to be more hawkish—more inclined to attack inflation aggressively—than their brethren at the board in Washington.

A number of economists have tried to quantify the relative independence of the major central banks. In practice, the independence of a central bank hinges on qualitative factors such as whether
politicians and the public respect the competence of the bank officials. But most academic measures of independence focus on more
quantifiable legal distinctions. In his introductory textbook (coauthored with Robert Frank) Bernanke approvingly notes that the Fed
ranks well on four criteria:[6]

1. Fed officials have relatively long appointments. Fed governors serve fourteen-year, staggered terms, compared with
   two, four, or six years for politicians.

2. The Fed does report to Congress periodically, but its daily
   policy actions are not subject to review by other branches
   of government.

3. The Fed does not have any obligation to finance budget
   deficits.

4. The Fed is self-financing through interest earned on its
   portfolio of government securities, and therefore is not
   obliged to submit requests for funding.

POLITICAL PRESSURE POINTS:
THE FED FEELS THE HEAT

Congress and the administration do, however, exert a subtle—and
sometimes not so subtle—pressure on the Fed through public warnings, breakfast meetings, letters requesting information, and testimonies before Congressional committees. The chairman now has a
regular schedule of four testimonies per year to Congress—to the
House and Senate banking committees in winter and summer, and
to the Joint Economic Committee of Congress in spring and fall.

Although the implicit threat of denying reappointment of the
chairman could be used to influence the Fed, in practice, presidents have proved to be very reluctant to invoke this prerogative.

Paul Volcker, a Democrat, was reappointed by the Republican Reagan. Greenspan, a Republican, was reappointed by the Democrat Clinton. George W. Bush reappointed Greenspan, even though his father, President George H. W. Bush, blamed Greenspan's reluctance to ease policy for his failure to win reelection in 1992. Still stinging from the loss, the older Bush had told a television interviewer in 1998 "I reappointed him and he disappointed me."[7] True, Volcker was not reappointed by Reagan a second time in 1987, despite having more time left in his governorship, but by most accounts Volcker could have had the appointment had he demanded it.[8]

Congress wants to be sure it understands what the Fed is doing and what is happening in the economy and financial markets. However, most of the chairman's time at Congressional testimonies is spent listening to very long statements that end with a brief question. Moreover, the topics often have nothing to do with monetary policy or the macro economy.

There seems to be a tradition where one of the populist congressmen takes the lead in criticizing the Fed. Perhaps the Fed's greatest critic was Wright Patman (D-Tex.), who served in the House from 1928 to 1976. According to Greider, Patman "devoted nearly fifty years in Congress to methodically assaulting the Federal Reserve and its privileged powers."[9] In the populist tradition, Patman believed the Fed was part of a conspiracy to help bankers and the rich at the expense of farmers, workers, and small businessmen.

When Patman died, the mantle shifted to another Democratic congressman from Texas, Henry Gonzalez (1961–1999). Gonzalez embarked on a campaign to open up the secretive Fed and, in the process, undercut its independence. Among his more aggressive proposals: impeach Volcker and broadcast FOMC meetings on TV. I was pulled into this dragnet when working as a corporate secretary at the Federal Reserve Bank of New York. Congressman Gonzalez had asked for the board of directors meeting minutes for each of the twelve Reserve Banks, and a group of us set about compiling those minutes and redacting any confidential personnel matters. Gonzalez was hoping to uncover some dark conspiracies at the Fed. What he found was what I already knew: these board meetings were boring affairs (frankly, in authoring a couple of years' worth of minutes, my creative writing skills were being underutilized).

More recently Jim Bunning (R-Kent.), Ron Paul (R-Tex.), and Barney Frank (D-Mass.) are the main critics of the Fed. Bunning was the only senator to oppose Bernanke's appointment to the Fed chair. Paul regularly introduces legislation calling for the abolishment of the Federal Reserve and a return to something akin to the gold standard. And Frank is more in the traditional mold of Fed critics: his main concern is that, by focusing too much on fighting inflation, the Fed is creating unnecessarily high unemployment and greater income inequality. He has argued strongly against the Fed adopting an inflation target, arguing that it would diminish the importance of the full employment part of the Fed's dual mandate.

In some respects the pressure on the Fed has been useful in opening up an overly secretive organization. Under Greenspan, the Fed invited criticism by acting as though it had something to hide. Many of the changes in Fed transparency in the 1990s—such as releasing the transcripts of meetings and releasing clear announcements of policy changes—were long overdue. While broadcasting FOMC meetings on TV was rightly rejected (it would have a chilling effect on policy discussions at the meetings, pushing the real decision making into the back rooms), it did make considerable sense to require the Fed to release meeting transcripts with a five-year lag. An even more obvious reform was Greenspan's decision to release a directive after each meeting, announcing any policy change. After all, why force financial firms to hire an expert in bank reserves to decipher whether the Fed has changed its funds rate target?

Just like the economy, political pressure on the Fed has both cycles and trends. When the Fed is fighting inflation, pressure mounts, especially in an election year. When the economy and the markets are humming along, on the other hand, politicians ignore the Fed.

Over the past twenty-five years, political pressure on the Fed has been declining. The peak in anti-Fed rhetoric was during Paul Volcker's war on inflation from 1979 to 1982. Breaking the back of double digit inflation required a double recession—the mini recession of 1980 and the major downturn of 1981–1982. During this period the Fed was under constant assault.

It was assailed by Congress:

- The leading Republican in the Senate, Howard Baker (R-Tenn.), held regular meetings with Volcker, urging lower interest rates.

- The leading Democrat in the Senate, Robert Byrd (D-Va.), proposed legislation forcing the Fed to ease.

- A resolution was passed urging the Fed to reevaluate the use of monetary targets.

- Senator Dennis DeConcini (D-Ariz.) opined that Volcker had "almost single-handedly caused one of the worst economic crises" in American history.[10]

- Representative Jack Kemp (R-N.Y.) demanded Volcker's resignation.

It was targeted by popular protest:

- Homebuilders put stamps on blocks of wood and mailed them to the Fed.

- Farmers on tractors circled the Fed building in Washington.

- The Homebuilders Association of Kentucky created "wanted" posters for each of the seven Fed governors.

- Groups representing homebuilders, retailers, and auto dealers mailed in keys to the Fed symbolizing lost business.

Members were even threatened with violence, both literal and figurative:

- A deranged person entered the Fed with a plan to take the governors hostage.

- Senator Mark Andrews (R-N.D.) told Volcker, "You're high on the hit parade for a lynching."[11]

Talk about pressure!

With the 1980 election out of the way and the economy on the mend, the pressure on the Fed eased in the mid-1980s. The Reagan administration did not have a clear strategy vis-à-vis the Fed. Reagan himself seemed to buy into Milton Friedman's view that, as long as the Fed was keeping growth in the money supply under control, they were doing their job. Among his economic advisers the focus was on supply-side economics and the virtues of tax cuts. Monetary policy was a sideshow compared with the alleged stimulative powers of tax cuts. Election-year pressure on the Fed was low during Reagan's presidency because the economy was in good shape during his reelection campaign in 1984.

The senior Bush presidency was an entirely different matter. There was almost no letup in pressure on the Fed from his successful election campaign in 1988 to his failed reelection campaign four years later. There were three reasons for this. First, Bush did not like the Fed's independence, and could not understand why Greenspan—a Republican—was unwilling to bend to political pressure. Second, members of Bush's economic policy team implicitly rejected the modern model of inflation: they believed that the Fed could juice the economy up, and then, if inflation accelerated, could simply take back the eases and inflation would go away at no cost. As we have seen, this ignores the legacy of higher inflation expectations. Third, and most important, Bush took over at a bad time for the economy.

By 1988 the Reagan economic boom was running out of steam, just as inflation pressures were emerging (figure 4-3). As inflation trended higher the Fed gently applied the brakes. The economy stumbled into recession in 1990 when Saddam Hussein's invasion of Kuwait and a spike in oil prices crushed consumer confidence. Even worse, going into the 1992 campaign the normal postrecession boom failed to materialize. Clinton's election mantra, "It's the economy, stupid," paid off. Growth finally started to pick up in the fall of 1992, but it was too late for Bush.

The Bush administration, from the top down, hectored the Fed to ease policy. In 1988 Bush the presidential candidate offered a

FIGURE 4-3

Unemployment and inflation, 1987–1993

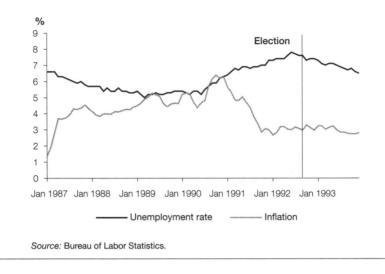

———— Unemployment rate   ———— Inflation

Source: Bureau of Labor Statistics.

word of caution to the Fed: "I would not want to see them step over some line that they would ratchet down, tighten down on economic growth."[12] During the transition to his new presidency, Bush again urged, "I do not want them to move so strongly against the fear of inflation that we impede growth."[13] In 1989 Bush's budget director Dick Darman, appearing on *Meet the Press*, gave a broader warning to the Fed: "It is important to not merely Chairman Greenspan but the other members of the board and the FOMC . . . that they be more attentive to the need to avoid tipping this economy into recession."[14] In his 1991 State of the Union message Bush was even more emphatic: "Interest rates should be lower now."[15] In 1992 Bush told the *New York Times*, "I'd like to see another lowering of interest rates."[16]

THE TIDE TURNS

During Bill Clinton's presidency, pressure on the Fed started out mild and then virtually disappeared. After the election there was an eleven-month honeymoon period where the executive branch ignored the Fed. In the face of a surprisingly slow economic recovery, the Fed had been on hold with just a 3 percent funds rate since the end of 1992. Then in December 1993, as the Fed started to hint at rate hikes, administration officials initially pushed back. According to Clinton, "There's no indication that we're facing a return of inflation." He added that until the economy produced "some real threat of inflation, it would be inappropriate for us to choke off an economy that has already had a false start or two" since the 1990–1991 recession had ended.[17] However, the push-back was mild. "The real question is not whether interest rates go up, but when and how much," admitted Frank Newman, undersecretary of the Treasury for Domestic Finance.[18] By January 1994, Treasury Secretary Lloyd Bentsen acknowledged that he expected rates to rise.

When Robert Rubin became Treasury secretary in 1995, the mild pressure on the Fed gave way to an official hands-off policy. Rubin argued that both the economy and financial markets would perform better if the Fed was left alone to do its job. President Clinton embraced the idea, asking, "Does anyone in his right mind think we would do anything to change the independence of the Fed?"[19]

Despite his father's problems with Greenspan, George W. Bush also embraced the hands-off policy. At his first meeting with Greenspan after the election Bush said, "I have full confidence in the Federal Reserve and we will not be second-guessing your decisions."[20] This was no idle promise. The Bush administration remained quiet through seventeen consecutive rate hikes, including three by untested rookie Bernanke. More recently the White House has remained silent even as the financial press has criticized the Fed for poor communication and failure to recognize the depths of the problems in capital markets.

THE STATE OF PLAY

Today the Fed is as strongly independent as it has ever been. No doubt there is still a steady undercurrent of political pressure on the Fed: members of Congress are not shy about giving advice to the Fed, and the chairman is frequently called in to talk to individual members and key committees. But for more than a decade, spanning two presidencies and six Treasury secretaries, and through several tightening cycles, there has been virtually no overt pressure on the Fed from the executive branch. Moreover, the number and virulence of congressional critics has steadily faded. Despite the ambiguous legal structure of the Fed, in reality it has become a very strong, very independent institution.

5

Blowing Smoke

The Fed's Evolving
Communication Strategy

Greenspan's term at the Fed saw not only a steady decrease in political pressure, but a closely related evolution in the way central banks communicated with the public. In the past, central bank communication could be described as "blowing smoke": the bankers were purposefully ambiguous about their policy actions and economic forecasts. Starting in the late 1980s, however, "no-smoking" rules began to appear at many of the major central banks. As I will show, it is not coincidence that clearer communication and reduced political pressure developed more or less simultaneously: a decline in political attacks on central banks made it easier for central bankers to be open about what they were attempting to do; at the same time, open communication with the public encouraged greater trust in the central bank. And Alan Greenspan was a relatively reluctant participant in this quiet revolution.

Blowing smoke, or more positively, *constructive ambiguity*, had been the norm in central banking for at least a century. Before

World War II, Sir Montague Norman, governor of the Bank of England, was the world's most powerful central banker. Asked for the reasons for his decision he replied, "Reasons, Mr. Chairman? I do not give reasons. I have instincts."[1]

A similar tradition has existed on this side of the Atlantic. Mervyn King, the current governor of the Bank of England, once asked Greenspan's predecessor, Paul Volcker, if he had "advice for a new central banker. He replied—in one word—'mystique.' "[2] With the Fed under intense—and often unfair—political pressure, Volcker would puff on a cigar while delivering a complicated—some would say, deliberately confusing—testimony to Congress. He "would lead a hostile questioner deeper and deeper into the esoterica of monetary policy until the embarrassed senator was lost in confusion."[3] After questioning Volcker at a hearing in 1980, one congressman remarked, "You would make an excellent prisoner of war because you would not tell the enemy anything."[4] Volcker and the other governors also spoke "in the dry and cautious language of economics, technical talk that was not very quotable. Their pronouncements were usually hedged with dangling qualifiers and framed in euphemisms that required an expert to translate."[5] (I can only hope this book has broken that pattern of communication!)

Of course, smoking at the Fed goes back much further than Paul Volcker. Arthur Burns, Fed chairman from 1970 to 1978 and a mentor of Alan Greenspan, would also surround himself with smoke, favoring a pipe rather than a cigar. Before Burns became chairman, the Fed had released transcripts of FOMC meetings with a five-year lag, providing an inside look at Fed deliberations. Under Burns, however, concerned about having to turn over documents more quickly under the new Freedom of Information Act, the Fed simply stopped keeping transcripts.

CONSTRUCTIVE AMBIGUITY

Greenspan continued the habit of constructive ambiguity when he became Fed chair in 1987. In his otherwise flattering biography,

Woodward describes "a tendency toward convoluted prose and wandering sentences," noting that Greenspan may have seen "the value of obscuring the message, particularly if your own conclusions and sentiments were not clear or were best not revealed." Woodward concludes: "The result was a verbal caution that could be maddening, a series of loose boards and qualifications in sentences that would allow him an exit ramp from nearly everything he said."[6]

Greenspan favored code words over direct statements. Former Fed governor Laurence Meyer says, "Reading the Chairman's speeches and testimony was a bit like reading the children's book *Where's Waldo?*"[7] Indeed, deciphering Greenspan's verbal gymnastics was a key part of my job. When speeches were released, I'd stand on the trading floor scanning the headlines from the wire services for the zinger headline. Then, with several members of my team, I would speed-read the speech, looking for anything the reporters had missed. I would tell clients, "One of my most prized possessions is my Greenspan decoder ring."

In central banking circles Greenspan's approach was sometimes called "policy by code word." For central bank watchers the game was as follows. First, the central bank would introduce a new code word without explaining exactly what it meant. Economists would then dig through the dictionary and history of previous policy statements to guess the hidden message. Initially, there might be considerable controversy about the exact meaning. But if the central banker repeated the phrase several times, and each time the same policy action followed, then the phrase is added to the code book. Under Greenspan, the classic example was in 2004 and 2005 when tightening at a "pace that is likely to be measured" came to mean "a 25-basis-point rate hike at every meeting." In Europe, a similar theme played out with the phrase "strong vigilance" on inflation. With repetition it came to mean: "We are probably raising rates within a month."

Greenspan was also deliberately vague in making forecasts for the economy and in explaining the goals of monetary policy. While he was famous for calling the upturn in productivity growth in the late 1990s, he never gave a number or even a range of possible estimates for the new improved trend. He also refused to put any kind of number on the key policy parameters. What is the Fed inflation goal? His answer: price stability is best thought of as an environment in which inflation is so low and stable it does not materially enter into the decisions of households and firms. What is the neutral rate for the funds target? His answer: when we arrive at neutral we will know it.

Greenspan's policy of constructive ambiguity became so well established he could joke about it in congressional hearings. Consider the following Yogi Berra–style head-scratchers: "If I seem unduly clear to you, you must have misunderstood what I said"; "I have learnt to mumble with great incoherence"; "I spend a substantial amount of my time endeavoring to fend off questions and worry terribly that I might end up being too clear"; "I'm trying to think of a way to answer that question by putting more words into fewer ideas than I usually do."[8] That Congress was willing to laugh along with these ironic comments shows how ingrained constructive ambiguity had become.

OH WHAT A TANGLED WEB:
THE PROS AND CONS OF AMBIGUITY

Why keep intentions hidden? Ben Bernanke argues that central bankers believed ambiguity made policy more effective: "Many central bankers of Norman's time (and, indeed, well into the postwar period) believed that a certain mystique attached to their activities and that allowing the public a glimpse of the inner workings would only usurp the prerogatives of insiders and reduce, if not grievously damage, the effectiveness of policy."[9] The money and banking textbook I used in the early 1980s suggested ambiguity was a natural defense mechanism: "A central bank concerned with its own survival and prestige has an incentive not to commit itself publicly to precise and highly visible targets, because if it has clear-cut, readily observable targets it would face criticism if it misses them."[10] On a similar note, one of Greenspan's biographers argues: "The Fed is positioned smack in the center of some major conflicts that run through American history: big government versus local control, elite banking versus agrarian interests. Therefore muddle and mystification are hallowed Fed strategies for keeping critics at bay."[11] According to one Greenspan critic, "Fedspeak allows the Fed speaker to claim credit or avoid blame, with equal plausibility, when policies or pronouncements turn out well or badly. That's what's constructive about the ambiguity. Fedspeak is a strategy that preserves not only the independence of the Federal Reserve but also the reputation of its chairman."[12]

In his memoirs, Greenspan presents only one argument for constructive ambiguity: it was good for efficient capital markets. He writes, "The Federal Reserve, in the interest of economic stability, had long sought to foster highly liquid debt markets through the use of what we called 'constructive ambiguity.'"[13] In particular, uncertainty about "the direction of interest rates would create a desired large buffer of both bids and offers."[14] In other words, if some traders believed Greenspan was signaling a tightening and others thought he was signaling an easing, there would be active, liquid markets as traders placed their bets. In his view, the move toward greater transparency that started in the early 1990s was possible because markets had become more liquid and having a more predictable policy "was seen as stabilizing the debt markets."[15]

If this argument sounds a bit obscure, it is. I am not a big fan of constructive ambiguity. Here I will only note some skepticism about Greenspan's explanation. The United States has the deepest, most liquid debt markets in the world—this was the case in the 1980s, and it is the case today. With the massive budget deficits of the 1980s, the U.S. Treasury market was particularly liquid. Why would the market melt down if Greenspan was clear? Arguing reductio ad absurdum, Greenspan is suggesting that central banks in other countries, with much less liquid markets, should have created the desired buffer of bids and offers by intentionally flip-flopping on their policy guidance.

In my mind, Greenspan's embrace of constructive ambiguity was a natural outcome of his background. He had travelled in politically charged circles for many years before becoming Fed chairman, working on a number of political campaigns and heading the Council of Economic Advisers (CEA) during the contentious post-Watergate years. According to Justin Martin it was at the CEA that Greenspan "first learned to equivocate before Congress."[16] He adds, "Greenspan, in fact, would practice in front of the CEA staff before appearing before Congress."[17] Fellow CEA member Paul MacAvoy recalls, "To prepare for public appearances, he used to try and say something and make it take the longest possible way to parse it out."[18] When he took the Fed chairmanship, Greenspan faced a similar environment of constant criticism from both the outside (Congress and the administration) and from inside the Fed (the committee had several outspoken mavericks). This was not an environment that encouraged an open exchange of ideas.

A RELUCTANT TRANSITION
TO TRANSPARENCY

Before 1994 the FOMC did not release any information after its meetings. Greenspan felt that an "immediate release of the directive [simply announcing whether rates were falling or rising] could threaten to roil markets unnecessarily, and concern about market reaction could reduce flexibility in decision making."[19] Instead, the markets had to guess what the Fed was doing based on whether the Fed was injecting more or less reserves into the banking system than expected. This guessing game was a jobs program for economists, obliging each major financial firm to hire a specialist in the obscure art of forecasting bank reserves.

Starting in the early 1990s, Greenspan slowly, and reluctantly, started to open up the Fed. At the February 1994 FOMC meeting Greenspan agreed—on a one-time basis only—to release a policy directive at the end of the meeting. He was concerned that Fed watchers would do the math wrong and misunderstand whether the Fed was hiking rates. This little glimmer of transparency was such an obvious success that the practice became permanent. Today the Fed releases a one page directive after each meeting, explaining its interest rate decision and giving hints about future policy. In addition to the policy directives, the Fed began to release more information, including releasing the minutes of meetings more quickly (figure 5-1).

Along the way, the Fed even had its own mini-version of the Nixon tapes—albeit without the swearing or the eighteen-minute gap. In the fall of 1993, members of the FOMC (and Congress) became aware that the tape recordings of FOMC meetings were being preserved (rather than destroyed once the minutes were published). Under pressure from Congress, in February 1995 the FOMC agreed to return to its pre-1970 practice of releasing verbatim transcripts, with a lag of five years. The transcript is complete, except for redactions of confidential material relating to individual firms, central banks, and foreign governments. Today, published transcripts are available for all FOMC meetings from 1979 through 2001.

Thus, inadvertently, the Fed now provides the most complete meeting records of any central bank. What does this big window into the secretive FOMC reveal? If conspiracy theories of the Fed were correct, the transcripts should have revealed some interesting backroom dealing, including hints of political influence, discussion

FIGURE 5-1

Increased transparency under Greenspan

November 1993	Begin releasing transcripts with five-year lag
February 1994	Start announcing policy changes
May 1999	Issue statement even if no change; reveal policy bias
February 2000	Indicate whether growth or inflation is greater risk
March 2002	Add vote to directive
May 2003	Separate up/down risk for growth and inflation
August 2003	Forward-looking language*
February 2004	Release minutes before, not after, next meeting

* "Considerable period" September, October, December 2004; "patient in removing" February, March 2004; "measured" May 2004 to December 2005; and "inflation risks remain" June 2006 to January 2007.

of the impact of policy on income distribution, and attempts to manipulate the markets. Instead, the transcripts offer—to quote William Greider—"the dry and cautious language of economics, technical talk that was not very quotable."[20] It turns out that once the smoke has cleared the "Temple" is not all that interesting, and does not really have any secrets.

PART II

BERNANKE'S BENCHMARK

The Shadow of Alan Greenspan

What is the outlook for the Bernanke Fed? In particular, how will Bernanke fare relative to the iconic benchmark, Alan Greenspan? To answer this question, the first step is to do a candid appraisal of Greenspan's successes and his failures. A couple of chapters will not do full justice to Greenspan's nineteen-year career at the Fed. However, like curing a bad golf swing, to understand Bernanke, investors must break the habits learned from almost two decades of watching Greenspan—old habits that have already produced some wrong reads.

Greenspan, I will show, had an enviable record in guiding the economy and financial markets. However, the mystique around

Greenspan is overblown. To err is human: Greenspan had his share of policy and forecasting errors, and in some ways the Fed lagged behind other central banks in terms of its communication strategy. In the blogosphere and op-ed world, Greenspan is eviscerated for failing to stop "serial bubbles" in the stock and housing markets and for endorsing President George W. Bush's 2001 tax cut. I will argue that while Greenspan deserves some criticism, the mistakes he made were more subtle and less egregious than the critics suggest. I hope through this portrait of Greenspan to put his legacy and Bernanke's inheritance into a realistic perspective.

6

Greenspan, an Enviable Record

Greenspan's Successes as Fed Chairman

When Greenspan assumed the Fed chairmanship he faced the same skepticism as Bernanke did about his ability to do the job. Investors asked, How could Greenspan possible fill the shoes of the larger-than-life (and 6 foot 7) Paul Volcker? While the markets sold off sharply on the announcement of Volcker's resignation; on sober reflection they recovered with Greenspan's appointment.

Greenspan came to the job with an excellent pedigree. His firm, Townsend-Greenspan, was a highly regarded economic consulting firm. He had served as an economic adviser to a number of leading Republican politicians. Under President Ford, he was head of the top economic advisory group to the president, the Council of Economic Advisors (CEA). In the early 1980s, he chaired the National Commission on Social Security Reform, which, while it did not quite solve the Social Security crisis, at least postponed it for thirty years. The only thing missing in his background was research or experience in the art of central banking.

By all accounts Greenspan had evolutionary, not revolutionary, changes in mind when he stepped into the job. Two immediate moves were obvious. First, as the world's consummate economic data junkie, Greenspan immediately upgraded the Fed's efforts in collecting anecdotal and industry data. Second, as a longtime Washington insider, he believed being independent in action did not mean avoiding meetings with politicians. In his memoirs Greenspan recounts an incident where Volcker had said it would be "inappropriate" for President Reagan to meet him at the Fed. Greenspan writes, "I was perplexed: I did not see how a visit by the president could compromise the Fed's independence."[1]

Aside from these changes, Greenspan continued on the path the Fed was already on. As we have seen, he continued the policy of constructive ambiguity in speaking with Congress and the public. He accepted that the Fed was in the business of trading off the risks of recession and inflation. Despite being a disciple of Ayn Rand's ultra–laissez faire philosophy, he embraced an active role for the Fed in managing the economy and financial crises.

POP CULTURE ICON I AM

In the latter half of his chairmanship, Greenspan became the rock star of the economic and financial world. Former Fed governor Laurence Meyer recounts that when Alan Greenspan entered his reconfirmation hearing with the Senate Banking Committee, "the Committee nearly genuflected. They heaped praise on the Chairman and weighed every word he uttered."[2] A&E Biography named Greenspan the "most fascinating person of 1999." In his book about Greenspan, Bob Woodward writes: "With Greenspan we find comfort. He helps breathe life into the vision of America as strong, the best, invincible . . . Each of us is a character in the nation's great economic soap opera; Greenspan is both director and producer."[3] In another biography, Justin Martin describes Greenspan as "an American first—a celebrity Fed chairman."[4]

This rock-star status owed much to growing public awareness of the importance of the Fed in managing the economy. People had learned that their jobs depended on Fed actions. This lesson was brought vividly to life by Paul Volcker's successful frontal assault on inflation. Tight Fed policy pushed the unemployment rate up to 10.8 percent in 1982, and easing Fed policy brought the unemployment rate back down to 6 percent by 1987. When Volcker resigned, the New York Times reported that "Mr. Volcker was considered almost a national hero for chopping inflation from an average rate of 12.8 percent in 1979 and 1980 to less than one-third that level."[5]

The public also became aware of the limits of fiscal policy. Part of the problem is that the legislative process is so cumbersome changes in taxes and expenditures occur too slowly to manage the ups and downs of the economy—often by the time an anti-recession tax cut is passed, the recession is over. Besides, after years of large budget deficits and politically motivated fiscal policy, the public worried that politicians could not be trusted to manage the economy. By contrast, the boring technocrats at the Fed seemed to know what they were doing. Hence, in the early 1980s US News & World Report elevated Volcker from sixth to second in its list of the most powerful men in America. Greenspan inherited that mantle.

Despite the initial doubts about Greenspan, by the end of his term, he had easily surpassed Volcker in terms of both popularity and celebrity status. When Greenspan stepped down from the chairmanship in 2006, an ABC News/Washington Post poll showed he had a 72 percent job approval rating, even though the same poll showed 60 percent of Americans rated the national economy negatively.[6]

TV reporting demands a face, and the Yoda-like Greenspan became symbolic of both economic and financial prosperity. Reporters often referred to Greenspan as a kind of shorthand for the Fed and the nineteen-member Federal Open Market Committee—in the public's mind, it was Greenspan who pulled the levers of policy and moved the markets with his Delphic views on the economy and the markets. Before Fed meetings, cameras would track the chairman's walk into the Fed building in Washington, speculating on what the size of his briefcase suggested for policy that day. (The supposition was that a thick briefcase was a sign that Greenspan was worried; a thin briefcase meant all was well. According to Greenspan's memoir, the thickness simply indicated whether he had packed a lunch that day!)[7] Greenspan much have relished the theater of striding up the stairs, because he could have easily avoided prying eyes by using the inside entrance (which the chairman has used for security reasons since the 9/11 attack).

Greenspan's prominent role in rescuing the markets in both 1987 and 1998 endeared him to investors. In February 1999 *Time* magazine put Greenspan on its cover (with Robert Rubin and Laurence Summers behind him) with the caption: "The Committee to Save the World."[8] His constant discussion of asset markets—stocks in the late 1990s and the housing market in the new millennium—was a reminder to investors that they had better pay attention. Right or wrong, when he commented on "irrational exuberance" or the "collective wisdom" of investors, his comments moved the market. He also became the poster child for the "New Paradigm" economy, with his early recognition of the improvement in labor productivity trends and his regular speeches on the topic.

THE GREAT MODERATION

Greenspan presided over and helped create a strong economy and strong financial markets. During his term inflation was nearly eliminated. Inflation is a lagging indicator, trailing shifts in both economic growth and monetary policy. Hence, in measuring success in the war against inflation for each Fed regime, it is best to measure the change in inflation from one year after the start of the term to one year after the end. By this measure, Arthur Burns and G. William Miller were miserable failures, adding 1.5 and 2.7 percent, respectively, to core personal consumption expenditures (PCE) inflation. By contrast Volcker sliced 4.7 percentage points off of the core, and Greenspan cut another 1.9 percent.[9]

How much credit should Greenspan get for the improvement? Ultimately, inflation is determined by central bank policy, but other political and economic forces can make inflation control easy or difficult. The failures of Burns and Miller were due in part to bad luck, but mainly to a lack of conviction—neither seemed to want to take responsibility for the required tough policy medicine. By contrast, Volcker attacked the problem head on. Under massive political pressure, facing inflation that had become deeply imbedded in the economy and the challenge of rising commodity prices, he declared war on inflation, driving it back to acceptable levels. War brings out greatness or failure—this is true both for the leader of a country and a leader of a central bank.

Greenspan's record as an inflation fighter was good, but not perfect. U.S. inflation roughly matched the European average during his chairmanship (figure 6-1). As I will discuss in detail later, Greenspan opposed announcing an official inflation target or goal for the Fed. However, in internal meetings he made it clear that he favored an unannounced target of 2 percent for the consumer price index (CPI).[10] He left office with core inflation hovering around 2 percent, down from just over 4 percent at the start of his chairmanship. However, CPI inflation averaged 3.1 percent during his tenure, meaning that, on average, the Fed overshot its informal target by about 1.1 percent.

Under Greenspan, the disinflationary path was greased in several ways. He faced a much less hostile environment than did Volcker. Political pressure on the Fed gradually faded over the course of his chairmanship. He also benefited from changes in the way inflation is measured. About a third of the slowdown in inflation over his tenure was the result of methodological changes in the construction of the CPI.[11]

Greenspan also benefited from a dramatic shift from adverse to positive supply shocks. Commodity prices surged until the early 1980s, creating both inflation pressures and imposing an "energy tax"

FIGURE 6-1

Inflation in the three biggest economies

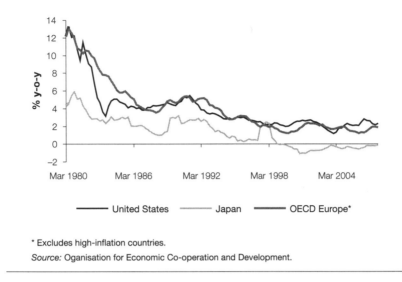

* Excludes high-inflation countries.

Source: Oganisation for Economic Co-operation and Development.

on consumers (higher prices diverted spending away from other uses). This meant a tough choice for the Fed: should it raise interest rates to damp consumer price inflation, or lower interest rates to offset the weakness in consumer spending? After rising much faster than overall consumer prices in the 1970s, commodity prices rose relatively slowly for much of Greenspan's chairmanship. The real price of commodities—that is, commodity prices divided by the consumer price index—was essentially flat from 1986 to 2002 (figure 6-2). On a similar note, after a long soft patch from 1973 to 1995, productivity growth surged during the second half of Greenspan's term. Strong productivity growth, particularly if unanticipated by workers, makes it easier to contain inflation, because gains in output per hour offset wage growth.[12]

Why did it take so long to get inflation down to the 2 percent goal? I believe this slow progress reflected Greenspan's passive approach to fighting inflation. Rather than trying to push inflation down, he favored *opportunistic disinflation*—that is, waiting for episodes of economic weakness or favorable supply shocks (such as

FIGURE 6-2

The real price of oil

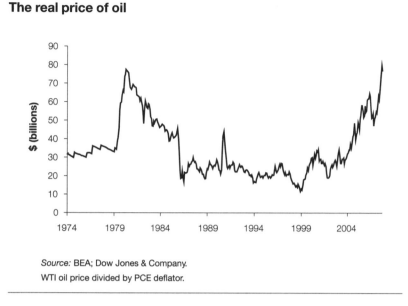

Source: BEA; Dow Jones & Company.
WTI oil price divided by PCE deflator.

lower oil prices) to lower inflation.[13] This way the Fed could lower inflation without actively imposing pain on the economy.

In his memoirs, Greenspan modestly credits the decline in inflation to global competition from China and other newly emerging economies. However, research from staff at the board of governors ascribes a few tenths of a percent of the fall in inflation to this competition.[14] In sum, Greenspan benefited from the disinflationary impact of weak commodity prices, strong productivity growth, and the emergence of low cost countries, but good monetary policy was probably the main reason for his good record on inflation.

Greenspan also presided over a period of very stable real economic activity. There were only two short and mild recessions during his tenure—eight-month-long recessions in both 1990–1991 and 2001. The economy was in recession for only 8 percent of his chairmanship. That compares with a 20 percent recession rate for the rest of the postwar period. Under Greenspan, Americans got used to the idea of a very stable business cycle, but this is far from the historic norm. In figure 6-3 the shaded areas mark

FIGURE 6-3

Industrial production and recessions

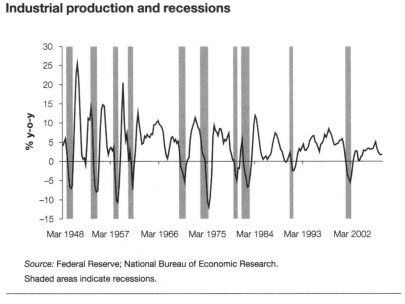

Source: Federal Reserve; National Bureau of Economic Research.
Shaded areas indicate recessions.

recessions and the chart gets a lot "darker" the farther one goes back in history.

There is an extensive literature on this great moderation, and Bernanke has weighed in on the subject. He argues that good luck played some role in the moderation: the same supply-side factors that contained inflation also contributed to growth stability. The moderation was also owing to structural changes: improved management of business inventories; the increased depth and sophistication of financial markets; deregulation in many industries; the shift away from unstable manufacturing toward more stable services; and increased openness to trade and international capital flows all may have increased macroeconomic stability. However, Bernanke's view is that "improvements in monetary policy, though certainly not the only factor, have probably been an important source of the Great Moderation."[15] The key to this success is the Greenspan Fed reacted strongly—or preemptively—to inflationary surges, thereby avoiding having to deliver even tougher medicine later.

RIDING TO THE RESCUE

From the public perspective, Greenspan's finest hours were during the inevitable financial earthquakes that struck during his term (figure 6-4). In 1987, only a few months into his rookie season as chairman, he faced the "Black Monday" stock market crash. That day the Dow Jones Industrial Average dropped 22.6 percent, marking the largest one-day percentage point decline in the history of the Dow. The Fed reacted by flooding the banking system with liquidity, and cutting its target for the federal funds rate by about 80 basis points. Greenspan also calmed the markets with a simple statement of support: "The Federal Reserve, consistent with its responsibilities as the Nation's central bank, affirmed today its readiness to serve as a source of liquidity to support the economic and financial system."[16] Greenspan's motto seemed to be "talk softly and supply a lot of liquidity." The efforts worked: the stock market stabilized and the economy continued to hum along.

FIGURE 6-4

Crises during Greenspan's tenure

1987	Stock market crash
1988–1990	Savings and loan crisis
1990	Stock market mini-crash
1990–1991	Gulf War I
1990–1991	U.S. recession
1994	Mexican peso crisis
1997	Asian financial crisis
1998	Russian debt crisis
1998	Long-Term Capital Management collapse
2000	Nasdaq collapse
2001	U.S. recession
2001	9/11 terrorist attack
2003	Gulf War II
2003–2004	Deflation scare

Greenspan was even more resolute around the collapse of Long-Term Capital Management in 1998. A financial crisis had been brewing for over a year, starting with the collapse in Thailand in July 1997, then spreading in domino fashion across Asia, then on to Russia, and finally landing on the shores of the United States in the fall of 1998. In each of these countries, policy authorities could not stop a collapse in investor confidence. In my writing at the time I referred to the crisis as a *financial freeze*, as one asset class after another became highly illiquid, and investors piled into the Treasury market. By September, not only had borrowing costs surged, but financial deals had ground to a halt. The Fed lowered interest rates by 25 basis points on September 30, and this was greeted with a Bronx cheer: "Is that the best you can do?" A second and third easing followed, however, and the markets steadily improved. As in 1987, the economy motored through the period oblivious to the carnage in financial markets.

I believe there are three reasons why Greenspan was so effective where other central bankers had failed. First, at the time these crises occurred, the U.S. economy was in good shape. From my vantage point as a Wall Street economist in both 1987 and 1998, it struck me that the market recovery was helped along by the release of data showing a healthy economy: with both the Fed and the economy supporting the market, investors began to wonder what all the panic was about. Second, Greenspan had the credibility that comes with running the world's premier central bank and that had been enhanced by his predecessor Paul Volcker. Finally, Greenspan had an effective "market-side" manner, talking to the markets and moving policy in a measured fashion that instilled confidence.

Of course, these market rescue operations came at a cost—moral hazard. *Moral hazard* is a term from the insurance business: it's the idea that if people have insurance they will take more risks, knowing that the insurance company will bail them out. For example, car insurance may make some drivers worry less about accidents, and thereby encourage more driving, or more dangerous driving. Similarly, by limiting the drop in the markets, the Fed may encourage excessive investor risk taking in the future. If investors know the Fed will always be there to bail them out, they may engage in ever more risky investment behavior. This moral hazard can contribute to the next financial bubble.

However, very few economists accept the "purge-the-rot" approach of simply stepping aside and letting the markets sort things out. I believe Greenspan did a reasonable job of balancing moral hazard with protecting the economy against financial crises. In the 1990s the moral hazard problem introduced the new term "the Greenspan put" into the financial lexicon. A "put" contract allows the buyer to sell an asset at a specified price—called the "strike price." This protects the owner of the asset from a big price drop because the owner has the option to sell at the agreed price. While there may have been a "Greenspan put" protecting investors, the "strike price" for this put was very low. That is the Fed did step in to help markets, but only after investors had suffered considerable pain and only if the financial meltdown threatened to put the economy into recession.

With a combination of luck and skill, Greenspan presided over a remarkably stable and healthy period for the U.S. economy. He was particularly adept in managing financial crises, striking a reasonable balance between bailing out investors and avoiding a recessionary shock. His success, combined with the growing fascination with the stock market and a growing recognition of the importance of the Federal Reserve, made him a pop culture icon. This is a tough legacy for any successor to live up to.

7

Greenspan, to Err Is Human

The Downside of Greenspan's Chairmanship

W hile there is little doubt that Greenspan was a strong Fed chairman, the hero worship in the business press got a little carried away.[1] A balanced appraisal requires asking some tough questions. Was Greenspan an anti-inflation hawk or easy-money dove? Should the Fed chairman work closely with the administration on issues unrelated to monetary policy and the regulation of financial markets? Should policy be communicated through ambiguous code words that only a professional Fed watcher could (usually) understand? Was Greenspan really a much better forecaster than other economists during his career? Was policy better with his domination of the FOMC?

BIRD-WATCHING: TELLING THE
ECONOMIC HAWKS FROM THE DOVES

Given the nerdy reputation of economists, it should come as no surprise to the reader that the most important job of a Wall Street economist is a form of bird-watching. Specifically, we "ornithoconomists" spend a good deal of time gauging the hawk or dove inclinations of Fed officials and Fed speeches. A *dove* tends to be soft on inflation and less inclined to hike interest rates. A *hawk* is tough on inflation and inclined to hike interest rates (and inflict pain on capital markets). How did Greenspan line up on the hawk-dove continuum?

It appears that as an inflation fighter, Greenspan was slightly to the dovish side of his contemporaries at the Fed and other central banks. How is that? The simplest gauge of the hawkishness of the chairman is to count up how many times other FOMC members strongly objected to a policy decision and lodged a formal dissenting vote. During Greenspan's tenure there were 83 dissenting votes at FOMC meetings, and hawkish dissents outweighed dovish dissents: 54 were for more hawkish action, 27 were for more dovish action, and 2 involved other issues (figure 7-1 shows dissents over an eighteen-year period). Behind the scenes there were considerably more informal dissents, with members grudgingly going along with the vote. For example, the transcripts for the 1994 tightening cycle show that there were only six formal dissents, but there were twenty-four cases in which members' pre-vote comments were in disagreement with the policy decision, with twenty of these expressing a preference for more aggressive action.[2]

There were at least two major episodes when Greenspan urged a more dovish path than the committee. First, in 1994, the majority of the committee preferred a 50-basis-point hike at the start of the cycle and repeatedly urged faster tightening along the way (although two new members, Alan Blinder and Janet Yellen, argued for restraint at the end of the cycle). As the transcript of the meetings shows, in a tour de force Greenspan convinced a majority of the committee to refrain from dissenting. Second, in the late

FIGURE 7-1

Dissenting votes at FOMC meetings

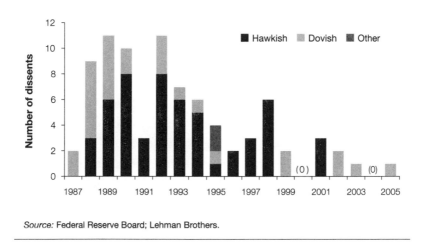

Source: Federal Reserve Board; Lehman Brothers.

1990s, Greenspan overrode the inflation concerns of the committee and the board staff, arguing that stronger productivity growth would contain inflation despite the low unemployment rate (his optimism proved correct).

In the second half of his term, Greenspan benefited from disinflationary tailwinds in the form of higher labor productivity growth, cheap imports from China and other emerging economies, and changes in the methodology for measuring inflation, all of which made it easier to control inflation without making the politically tough choice of raising interest rates. His policy of opportunistic disinflation worked well in this environment, and so at least some of his success may be a matter of luck: one wonders how he would have fared if faced with the challenges Paul Volcker inherited.

VIOLATING THE PRIME DIRECTIVE

For most central bankers and macroeconomists, the worst thing for a central bank is to lose its ability to make decisions independent of political pressure. In the science fiction series *Star Trek*, the prime directive for a starship captain is that there can be no interference with the internal affairs of other civilizations; it is not an overstatement to say the prime directive for Fed officials is to avoid political matters that unnecessarily risk the independence of the Fed.

Greenspan, like *Star Trek*'s Captain Kirk, often seemed to stretch the rules. Indeed, the biggest criticism of Greenspan from former Fed governors is that he allowed himself to be drawn into politically sensitive matters. Thus, in his book *A Term at the Fed*, Laurence Meyer writes, "Despite my admiration for the Chairman, I've had a few bones to pick." Meyer goes on to focus on Greenspan's violations of the prime directive, noting that "Greenspan's tendency to speak on issues that are beyond the authority of the Federal Reserve" threatened the Fed's independence and further remarking, "By inserting himself into the political debate about fiscal policy, the Chairman might encourage others in government to reciprocate by meddling in monetary policy."[3] On a similar note, former governor Alan Blinder, in a paper coauthored with Ricardo Reis, writes that "central bank independence is best thought of—and best preserved—as a two-way street. If Congress is supposed to stay out of monetary policy, then the Fed should stay out of fiscal policy and other political matters."[4]

How serious are these charges? At the outset, it is important to underscore that I have found no evidence that Greenspan's political links compromised his monetary policy actions. On the contrary, the evidence shows he ran a nonpartisan, independent monetary policy. Searching through the recent FOMC transcripts reveals no evidence of partisan politics. There is some evidence that the Greenspan Fed tried to keep a low profile in the months around elections, giving fewer speeches and attempting to avoid moving the funds rate up or down just before an election. However, there is no evidence that it did this to favor one political party or the other. In a paper we wrote in 2004 Joe Abate and I formally tested whether the Greenspan Fed acted differently during elections.[5] We estimated policy reaction functions—equations that predict where the funds rate will be, based on economic fundamentals. We found no evidence that under Greenspan the Fed operated any differently around elections, regardless of which party was in power. Indeed, if anything, the Greenspan Fed kept interest rates slightly higher than normal around elections.

Nonetheless, as Meyer and Blinder politely suggest, Greenspan did not merely put his toe over the line separating the Fed from the rest of the government, sometimes he leaped over it. Reading Greenspan's memoirs, I was impressed, but also a bit concerned, by his ubiquitous presence in most of the major economic policy decisions of his time. Despite the party differences, Greenspan worked very closely with the Clinton administration. In his memoirs, Greenspan says, "Rubin, Summers and me . . . became economic foxhole buddies."[6] Most important, he played a pivotal role in the Clinton administration's decision to focus on reducing the budget deficit.

Greenspan had even deeper ties to the George W. Bush administration, which included many "stalwarts" and friends from the Ford presidency.[7] These extended not only to economic and policy advice, but also to personnel decisions: he even called up Paul O'Neill to lobby him to accept the position of secretary of the Treasury. In his memoir he writes, "During the Bush Administration, particularly after 9/11, I spent more time at the White House than ever before in my Fed career . . . I was back being a consultant. The agendas of these meetings covered international economics, the global dynamics of energy and oil, the future of Social Security, deregulation, accounting fraud, problems with Fannie Mae and Freddie Mac, and, when appropriate, monetary policy."[8]

The rub is that there are many people who can serve as economic advisers to Congress and the executive branch, but the Fed chairman's role in this respect should be limited. Greenspan never seems to have asked himself, Is it appropriate for the chairman of an independent central bank to be an active consultant to the executive branch on hiring decisions and policy matters well outside the purview of the Fed? Are not there other economists who can perform this function, without the conflict of interest? Even if the Fed chairman can compartmentalize monetary policy separately from the economic consulting business—as Greenspan seems to have done—is it worth risking the appearance of partisanship?

2001, A TAX ODYSSEY: GREENSPAN'S ROLE IN THE BUSH TAX CUT

Possibly the most controversial moment of Greenspan's chairman-ship was when he seemed to endorse the Bush administration's 2001 tax cut, which has been criticized for bringing back budget deficits. The liberal press has severely criticized Greenspan's sup-port of the legislation. I believe the endorsement was a mistake, but I also believe his motives for supporting the cut were more subtle than simply helping out his Republican friends.

It is important to judge Greenspan according to the knowledge he would have had at the time, not with 20-20 hindsight. In 2001, virtu-ally every budget forecaster, including yours truly, was expecting large surpluses for many years to come (figure 7-2). Greenspan was simply restating the consensus when he pointed out that the surpluses could wipe out the public debt. Once the debt was paid off, the government would have three choices: raise spending; cut taxes; or use the ongo-ing surpluses to buy up large amounts of private assets.

FIGURE 7-2

Expected and actual budget balance

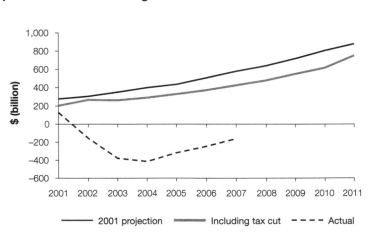

Source: Congressional Budget Office; Department of the Treasury.

For a conservative economist such as Greenspan, the only thing worse than bloating the size of government was the government buying lots of private-sector assets. He worried that such a "sovereign wealth fund" would be tempted to pick winners and losers in the markets, distorting capital flows.[9] The Congressional Budget Office was forecasting a surplus of $500 billion by 2006. Greenspan writes in his memoir: "I felt stunned: $500 billion is . . . roughly equivalent to the combined assets of America's five largest pension funds, piling up each year."[10] According to Bob Woodward, Greenspan believed this was "something that [had] got to be focused on very sharply and stated publicly, because no one had identified the problem. He decided it was time to cut taxes now to forestall the possibility of the government gaining control of so much money by becoming a giant potential investor in the stock market." What about perceptions of partisanship? Greenspan reasoned that "since nearly everyone seemed to be for some kind of tax cut, he was not taking sides or being partisan."[11]

The problem with Greenspan's action was not that he was abandoning his principled belief in low budget deficits. It really did look as if big surpluses lay ahead, and the fiscally conservative thing to do was cut taxes. Moreover, in his speeches Greenspan made clear that any tax cuts should be phased in and should have an escape clause should the surplus start to disappear. He suggested including "provisions that limit surplus-reducing actions if specified targets for the budget surplus and federal debt were not satisfied."[12]

The problem was that he unnecessarily thrust the Fed into the middle of a highly contentious political debate. Greenspan himself noted that both political parties favored some kind of tax cut, so why did he need to speak out to make sure the tax cuts happened? Moreover, he had fair warning that, despite his appeal for restraint, his endorsement would have exactly the opposite effect. Before Greenspan delivered his testimony, both Kent Conrad, the senior Democrat on the Senate Budget Committee, and former Treasury Secretary Rubin pleaded with him to withhold the endorsement. They argued that he would be throwing fuel on the fire, encouraging an even bigger tax cut. Rubin pointed out that the press would spin the testimony as direct support for the Bush plan.[13] Greenspan, the master of Washington politics and Fedspeak, responded to Rubin, "I can't be in charge of people's perceptions. I don't function that way."[14] Ironically, Greenspan entered the debate favoring a contained tax cut but, by giving the "Greenspan seal of approval," he undercut his own advice.

YOU'LL NEED A GREENSPAN
DECODER RING

The confusion over Greenspan's tax advice hints at another challenging aspect of Greenspan's chairmanship: his complicated system of communicating with the public. Under Greenspan, policy changes were often signaled through an evolving system of code words. He almost never gave specific forecasts for anything, and instead used descriptive language. Select members of the press and visitors to the Fed were often used as the conduit for delivering the message. At times Greenspan deliberately misstated the Fed view. While this helped keep professional Fed watchers like myself busy and well compensated, I have always believed that a clear, more direct approach would have been more effective.

As already noted in chapter 5, Greenspan also tended to speak in Delphic tones, often favoring ambiguous phrases. While Greenspan never talked about it, Fed officials had a number of reasons to be deliberately vague. It was a way to avoid giving ammunition to the critics and avoid strict accountability for forecast errors. With speeches loaded with qualifiers and with no concrete numbers, a broad range of economic or policy outcomes was consistent with some part of the message. It also discouraged investors from fixing on a view and misunderstanding the uncertainties underlying the economy and policy.

Not surprisingly, Greenspan's statements sometimes caused confusion. At times his "translators" would draw completely contradictory conclusions from his speeches. After one Greenspan speech in 1995, the *Washington Post* reported, "Greenspan Hints Fed May Cut Interest Rates," while the *New York Times* headline read, "Doubts Voiced by Greenspan on a Rate Cut."[15] At other times, Fed watchers read hidden messages that were not there, causing the markets to anticipate policy moves the Fed did not intend to make. As I noted above, Greenspan's endorsement of a moderate tax cut was almost universally reported as a go signal for a major tax cut. Similarly, in 2003, when Greenspan said the Fed needed to create a "firebreak" against deflation, it was widely interpreted as a signal of a big 50-basis-point interest rate cut; the actual 25 basis points cut weeks later caused a huge reversal in the bond market.

MISGUIDED MARKET MANAGEMENT

At times Greenspan also attempted to "constructively misguide" the markets. There are limits to how transparent the Fed should be. For example, the Fed needs to appear confident and in command during financial crises, to not cry "fire" when investors are heading for the exits. However, Greenspan sometimes tried to manage market expectations even in more normal times.

In doing so, Greenspan offered both tactical and strategic misdirections. The biggest strategic misdirection was to repeatedly assert that the Fed does not have a numerical objective for inflation. Back in 1996 Greenspan agreed on a 2 percent goal for CPI inflation—that fact was revealed when the FOMC transcripts were released in 2001. At a tactical level often he would try to game market expectations of Fed policy. For example, at the November 2000 FOMC meeting, with the markets beginning to anticipate a potential Fed easing, Greenspan argued that the Fed should not drop its tightening bias because "even if we believe that the risks are truly balanced as of today, the market does not believe that is our view. As a consequence, were we to go to balance today we would almost surely end up tomorrow with financial conditions that would be too easy in terms of the current outlook."[16] In other words he feared that investors would take out their "Greenspan decoder rings" and overreact, interpreting the move to neutral as an inevitable first step toward easing.

There are two problems with this lack of candor with the markets. First, it did not work very well. Economists and traders on Wall Street are well paid to see though smoke. Thus trying to guide the markets could work in limited instances, but only if new ways are found to fool investors. As the saying goes: fool me once, shame on you; fool me twice, shame on me. Indeed, this lack of clarity produced exactly the dynamic Greenspan was worried about in 2000: rather than take the Fed at its word, the market looks for hidden messages, with attendant overreactions and misreadings.

A second problem is that lack of candor undercuts the credibility of the Fed with the general public. Coded messages, constructive ambiguity, and attempts to manage market expectations contribute to a populist impression that the Fed has something to hide. The premise of William Greider's *The Secrets of the Temple* was that the Fed was this powerful institution that deliberately hid its actions and avoided public accountability. The Fed should not encourage that thinking.

JUDGMENT ERRORS

During his time as Fed chairman, Greenspan developed a reputation not only as the world's preeminent central banker, but also as its best economic forecaster. This reputation was based on his legendary knowledge of economic statistics. Few, if any, economists could match Greenspan's ability to dissect and connect government statistics, industry data, and anecdotal evidence.

Greenspan's reputation was made when he spotted the upturn in productivity growth in the mid-1990s much earlier than anyone else at the Fed. This was a very important call—the economic forecasting equivalent of a grand slam home run—because an acceleration in the growth in worker's output per hour had four secondary implications. First, by lowering business costs it meant the economy could grow faster without exacerbating inflation. Second, it explained the surge in profits, helping justify the stock market boom. Third, it helped justify the low saving rate: if productivity and income growth remained strong, people did not need to save as much to fund their future spending needs. And, most important, it gave the Fed breathing room to let the economy grow, without needing to constrain inflation.

It is worth noting, however, that this was the second time that Greenspan had predicted a productivity renaissance (figure 7-3 provides a perspective on movement in productivity). *Wall Street Journal* reporter Greg Ip notes that "Greenspan's productivity insight in 1996 had come to him in an earlier, less successful form."[17] Back in 1987 Greenspan argued that "productivity growth in many key nonmanufacturing areas of the economy, where high tech predominates, may have been significantly underestimated in recent years." If correct, this should have helped keep inflation at bay, and yet inflation surged during this period and the data still show very low productivity gains in this period.

FIGURE 7-3

Productivity growth

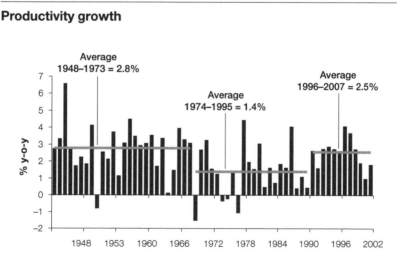

Source: Bureau of Labor Statistics.

It is difficult to judge Greenspan's overall forecast record during his chairmanship because he virtually never put a number on anything. He preferred ambiguous phrases that made it very difficult to prove him wrong. This applied even to his seminal call on the surge in productivity growth—productivity growth was higher than the feeble 1.4 percent trend of 1973 to 1995, but how much higher, he did not say. Looking back at key moments, sometimes he was ahead of the economic profession and sometimes behind. Consider three examples. Although we now know the economy dipped into recession starting in July 1990, at the August 21, 1990, FOMC meeting Greenspan said, "I think there are several things we can stipulate with some degree of certainty, namely that those who argue that we are already in recession . . . are reasonably certain to be wrong."[18] In 1996 he was probably a few years early in calling the stock market bubble, since even after the 2000–2001 crash the markets reversed the last couple years of the stock market boom but never came close to the 1996 level. On the other hand, Greenspan seemed a step ahead of the economics profession in spotting the weakness in the economy in the winter of 2000–2001, prompting a surprise 50-basis-point cut on January 4, 2001.

His forecast record as an economic consultant is easier to judge because the forecasts were a matter of public record. The evidence I have uncovered is not favorable. In 1984 his firm Townsend-Greenspan opened a money market business using Greenspan's analysis of economic cycles and trends. According to *Forbes* magazine, it turned in "one of the least impressive records of all pension fund advisors."[19] A more telling example came from a study by the Federal Reserve Bank of Boston. The study compared Townsend-Greenspan to seven other forecasting firms for the period 1976 through 1985. The firm was in the middle of the pack in predicting real GDP growth, but ranked last in terms of inflation forecasting.[20] From 1982 to 1986 it overestimated inflation every year by between 1.2 and 2.4 percentage points.

Claims of clairvoyance never came from Greenspan himself. Over the years he frequently joked about the forecast inaccuracy of economists, and he paid close attention to the role of forecast uncertainty in shaping policy choices. Indeed, knowing his own limits was one reason Greenspan avoided offering numerical forecasts and always heavily hedged his arguments with qualifiers and caveats. A fair assessment of Greenspan's forecasting record is that he was probably better than average at catching short-term twists in the data but, as with all economists, his medium- and long-term forecasts were spotty.

BENEVOLENT DICTATORSHIP
OR DEMOCRACY?

In theory the FOMC operates under a one man, one vote principle. In practice, particularly in the second half of his chairmanship, Greenspan dominated his committee. This shift in the balance of power took several forms.

At times he seemed to front-run his committee—hinting at a likely rate move to the markets and then presenting it as more or less a fait accompli to his committee—"the markets expect a move and we can't disappoint." The transcripts of FOMC meetings reveal considerable uncertainty about how much discretionary power the chairman had to make small policy changes without consulting the committee. Greenspan usually asked for a formal vote before making a policy move, but at times he stretched his power.

Greenspan discouraged dissenting votes at FOMC meetings. According to Bob Woodward, "There was a tradition at the Fed that members go along with the chairman unless they are really uncomfortable, terribly uncomfortable."[21] In his book *A Term at the Fed*, former governor Laurence Meyer describes a "game of musical chairs" at FOMC meetings.[22] He writes that more than two dissenting votes "would be disruptive to the process of monetary policy making and unsettling to financial market" hence members later in the voting queue would not dissent if two members had already dissented. Meyer also describes Greenspan's efforts to tone down the public statements of other members of the FOMC. At one meeting he asked members how they might increase discipline in public speeches. In response, one member said he tried to be boring; another said he commented only on things unrelated to Fed responsibilities. Meyer also says Greenspan wanted, but ultimately gave up on, issuing formal speaking guidelines for FOMC members.[23]

There are some advantages to having a dominant chairman. The FOMC is an inefficient decision-making body. With nineteen members, including twelve voters, the committee is too big. With nine and six members, respectively, the Bank of England and Bank of Canada are far more efficiently organized. Adding to the awkwardness is the Byzantine voting system where all governors and the New York president vote every year, but the other four votes rotate among the other eleven members on an annual basis. To move at a reasonable speed, the committee must delegate some power to the chairman.

If Greenspan was a dictator, he seemed like a benevolent one. Statistical tests show no evidence that monetary policy was politically motivated during his tenure. His flexible views of how the economy worked and his willingness to change course if the standard models were not working made it less likely that he would drift down a seriously misguided path.

However, there is a danger in having such a dominant leader. As Blinder and Reis argue, committee decisions have four advantages: (1) they are less volatile, (2) they provide insurance against an outlier view, (3) they pool knowledge, and (4) groups process information better than a highly skilled individual when faced with a complex task.[24] It is conceivable that Greenspan's skill may have so exceeded the average of his committee that his domination was optimal. However, with Greenspan's retirement, and given the mixed record of Fed chairmen over the years, continuing the "imperial chairmanship" would seem to be a mistake.

Finally, as with a number of my other criticisms of the former chairman, there is a dynamic cost to having a dominant chairman. If dissent and free speech are discouraged—and this was obvious to Fed watchers during Greenspan's tenure—then every tiny hint of disagreement takes on a much bigger meaning: more than one dissent is a sign of a major rift on the FOMC and a stray hawkish or dovish sentence in an otherwise purposely dull speech is a subtle signal of more aggressive Fed action. Hence when a new uninitiated member joined the FOMC—Laurence Meyer was a good example—the markets would often overreact to his speeches.[25] In the markets and in the press small disagreements were often blown out of proportion, suggesting secret power struggles within the institution.

A longer-term dynamic cost of a dominant chairman is that it may reduce the quality of the FOMC. If members of the committee do not feel they have a real influence on the decisions of the committee, they will make less effort. Having a dominant chairman also could discourage strong macroeconomists from joining the board—who wants to have a job rubber stamping decisions and giving deliberately uninteresting speeches? In a worst-case scenario, a self-reinforcing dynamic can develop where good people do not want to join the FOMC, making it even more important to have a strong, dominant chairman.

There are times—such as when the Fed is under major political attack or facing very fragile markets—when presenting a united face behind the chairman is vital. But other central banks, such as the Bank of England, retain the confidence of the government and financial markets despite close votes at policy meetings. Allowing some of the internal debate to spill over into the public shows that the Fed is a confident, intellectually vibrant institution facing highly uncertain choices.

LOTS OF FROTH: THE CONUNDRUM
OF FINANCIAL BUBBLES

There is one major area of Fed policy where I disagree with both Greenspan and Bernanke: their approach to suspected bubbles in asset markets. Both argue that the Fed should adopt an asymmetric approach: don't try to stop potential asset bubbles—they are too difficult to identify and control—but deal aggressively with the consequences if the boom leads to bust. I believe this hands-off approach to potential bubbles is too extreme. In my mind, a policy of leaning against asset bubbles should be just another of the risk-management aspects of central bank policy. Much more on this later.

Regardless of whether the Fed should or should not lean against bubbles, clearly the Fed should not be in the business of encouraging a potential bubble. I believe Greenspan inadvertently encouraged bubbles during his chairmanship. Despite his market savvy, at times Greenspan did not seem fully aware of how his commentary encouraged the stock market boom of the late 1990s and the more recent home price boom.

Greenspan was one of the first economists to spot the pick-up in productivity growth in the mid-1990s, and he never tired of talking about it. However, with his understanding of markets, he should have noticed that his "new paradigm" rap was dance music to the markets. For optimists in the stock market, talk of higher trend growth morphed into "there is no limit to growth." The idea that the business cycle had become less violent became "the business cycle is dead." A temporary surge in profits due to strong productivity (and lagging wage demands) became "a permanent trend of double-digit profit growth." A strong stock market with lower risk premiums became "Dow 36,000." And when the Fed finally attempted to cool off the economy at the end of the decade, this was interpreted as "good news for stocks because the Fed is engineering a soft landing."

Greenspan also may have encouraged asset bubbles by arguing that the rise in prices was justified by economic fundamentals or by denying that a bubble could be identified. While in 1996 Greenspan talked of possible "irrational exuberance" in the stock market, over time he became increasingly agnostic about whether there was indeed a stock market bubble. In January 1999 he said, "As I have testified before the Congress many times, I believe, at root, the remarkable generation of capital gains of recent years has resulted from the dramatic fall in inflation expectations and associated risk premiums, and broad advances in a wide variety of technologies that produced critical synergies in the 1990s."[26] In 1999 he also argued, "Bubbles generally are perceptible only after the fact. To spot a bubble in advance requires a judgment that hundreds of thousands of informed investors have it wrong. Betting against markets is usually precarious at best."[27] The stock market boom played little role in policy until 2000, when he warned, "With foreign economies strengthening and labor markets already tight, how the current wealth effect is contained will determine whether the extraordinary expansion that it has helped foster can slow to a sustainable pace."[28]

A similar pattern occurred with the housing market. In June 2005 Greenspan conceded that there is "froth in some local markets," but that the risks to the national economy were low.[29] He explained that the housing market is inherently resistant to speculative activity, that local markets are only "loosely connected," and that "while investors can arbitrage the price of a commodity such as aluminum between Portland, Maine, and Portland, Oregon, they cannot do that with home prices because they cannot move the houses. As a consequence, the behavior of home prices varies widely across the nation, and prices in Portland, Maine, do not affect prices in Portland, Oregon, [and so] for homeowners to realize accumulated capital gains on a residence—a precondition of a speculative market—they must move." He also noted that transactions costs were high: "Commissions and closing cost . . . average in the neighborhood of 10 percent of the sales price." His bottom-line: "Although we certainly cannot rule out price declines . . . these declines, were they to occur, likely would not have substantial macroeconomic implications."

With the benefit of 20-20 hindsight, this argument looks clearly wrong, but even at the time it seemed like a stretch. In our weekly meeting, responding to Greenspan's speech, Joe Abate and I argued that while local housing markets were normally relatively uncorrelated, in the hothouse environment of 2004 and 2005, local markets were connected by both the proliferation of easy credit and the growing class of speculative buyers.[30] While the two Portlands were not closely connected, there were growing signs of contagion in the western states and Florida. It seemed like more than a coincidence that home price inflation accelerated in all fifty-seven major metro areas in the West from 2003 to 2004. This growing psychological connection was important because it meant that these markets were more likely to rise and fall together, creating greater risk of an economic shock of national significance.

We also disputed Greenspan's view that homeowners would have to sell their homes to be affected by the speculative frenzy. Many households were realizing their gains by running down their other savings or using their houses as collateral for loans. Some households speculated by delaying selling their first home after buying a second home. Finally, transaction costs were a deterrent to speculation, but in many cases they had fallen to less than half of the 10 percent figure Greenspan cited. Our bottom line: there was a high risk of a synchronized price decline across many speculative markets, which would create a shock of national significance to the housing market and the economy.[31]

My advice to the Fed is simple. When asset markets are hot, don't add fuel to the fire by denying that a bubble exists or arguing that economic fundamentals are pushing up prices. Putting a new twist on an old expression: when it comes to a potential asset bubble, "If you don't have anything bad to say, don't say anything at all."

PULLING MY PUNCH: A TENTATIVE
BOTTOM LINE ON GREENSPAN

As I wrote this chapter, the idea of doing a point-by-point critique of Alan Greenspan felt almost blasphemous. It is impossible to do full justice to such a long career in just a couple of chapters. Surely Greenspan deserves a good deal of the credit for the strong performance of the economy and financial markets during his nearly twenty years at the helm. Over the years, I participated in a number of polls that asked for a letter grade for Greenspan. I never gave him less than a B, even in some of his rockier moments. After spending most of my professional career trying to put myself into Greenspan's shoes and guess his next move, it feels odd to focus on what he should have done instead of what he was likely to do.

Stepping back and seeing the broader picture, however, the man falls short of the heroic caricature often presented in the press. Like all central bankers, he had a mixed record in timing policy moves: sometimes he was ahead of his committee and the economic consensus and sometimes he was behind. Like all economists, he had a mixed forecasting record—economic forecasting is a humbling science. Sometimes his gut instincts served him well—identifying the productivity boom of the late 1990s—and sometimes his instincts were wrong—misidentifying the productivity boom of the late 1980s. He should take some of the blame for the two big asset bubbles that emerged during his term: by repeatedly saying bubbles can't be identified in advance he may have actually encouraged the bubbles. He clung too long to the old "blowing smoke" communication strategy. Perhaps his weakest moments were when he let his guru status get the better of him and he inserted himself into political matters unrelated to monetary policy. This chapter may sound a bit nit-picky; after all, the guy's only human. Exactly.

PART III

BERNANKE'S BELIEFS

How Bernanke's Life Work Shapes His Policies

While Alan Greenspan had a relatively limited agenda when he stepped into the Fed chairmanship, Bernanke was a bit more ambitious. After decades of research on monetary economics and several years as a Fed governor, he had developed a clear agenda.

So I'll first look at his foremost objective, moving toward adopting a target for inflation. It is no coincidence that one of Bernanke's first acts as chairman was to form a subcommittee to explore inflation targeting and other measures to improve communication. Second, I look at how his study of the Great Depression and of Japan's "lost decade" impacts his response to financial and economic turmoil. Third, I ex-plore changes in the Fed's operating style under Bernanke, including more reliance on models and staff research, less domination of the committee, and a more direct speaking style. Fourth, Bernanke's agenda is not all about change: I will look at how Bernanke planned to continue the Greenspan approach to potential asset market bub-bles. Finally I look at how his research motivates a risk-management approach during times of unusual stress.

8

Constrained Discretion

Bernanke's Quest for
an Inflation Target

One of the hot topics in monetary economics is whether policy makers should be constrained by rules or use discretion.[1] Advocates of discretion argue that the Fed should react to developments in the economy using its best judgment at the time. They believe that in a complicated and ever-changing world, rules prevent the Fed from correctly balancing risks to growth, inflation, and financial markets. By contrast, rules advocates argue that policy makers are not very adept at managing the economy, that they can be influenced by politicians, and that they may be tempted to pursue policies that boost economic performance in the short term at the expense of long-term economic stability. They also argue that a rules-based approach may increase the central bank's credibility, making it easier to meet long-run goals like low and stable inflation.

Bernanke clearly laid out the case for policy rules in a speech in 2004, pointing to work by Kydland and Prescott.[2] He noted,

"Monetary policy makers will generally find it advantageous to commit publicly to following policies that will produce low inflation. If the policy makers' statements are believed (that is, if they are credible), then the public will expect inflation to be low, and demands for wage and price increases should accordingly be moderate. In a virtuous circle, this cooperative behavior by the public makes the central bank's commitment to low inflation easier to fulfill."[3] Simply put, if the public believes the Fed will keep inflation low, then individuals will be less likely to raise their own wages or prices when the economy heats up or costs rise because they have faith that the Fed will resist those inflationary pressures. The Fed will not have to impose as much pain on the economy to maintain or lower inflation.

Rules advocates used to focus on the case for targeting money growth. In the 1970s, with inflation running at double-digit rates, many central banks adopted money targets. In the United States, the Full Employment and Balanced Growth Act of 1978 required the Fed to set one-year target ranges for money supply growth twice a year and to report the targets to Congress. Initially, the Fed focused on a narrow definition of money called "M1," which was simply cash plus checking accounts. Over time, however, new assets were developed that could be used like a checking account, such as money market funds, and these were added into a broader definition of money called "M2." The hope was that the public would see the link between low money growth and low inflation, making it easier for the Fed to lower inflation. The new law required that the Fed chairman report back twice a year to Congress on the new policy. This reporting was called the Humphrey-Hawkins testimony after the bill's sponsors, Senator Hubert Humphrey (D-Minn.) and Representative Augustus Hawkins (D-Cal.).

Unfortunately, the money growth targets were generally a failure. The problem was that financial innovation blurred the line between money (liquid assets such as cash and checking accounts) and illiquid savings. For example, an interest-paying money market fund is a lot like a checking account, but it is also a very safe form of saving. If money market funds are growing rapidly, does this mean there is a lot of money or liquidity in the economy, facilitating

FIGURE 8-1

Money and GDP growth

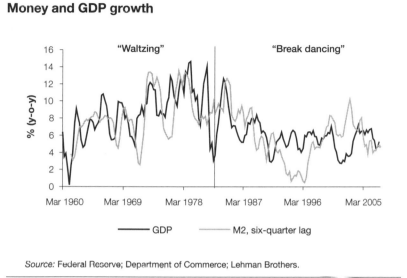

Source: Federal Reserve; Department of Commerce; Lehman Brothers.

spending and suggesting inflation risks? Or is it a sign that investors are seeking safe investments, suggesting a weak spending climate and low inflation? Until the early 1980s, statistical tests showed that surges in money growth were followed—with a one- or two-year lag—by surges in nominal GDP growth (figure 8-1). By contrast, in the last twenty-five years or so, strong money growth has been associated—with a lag—with slower GDP growth. Ironically, just as the money targets were being adopted, the relationship between money growth and the economy became very unstable. As Gerald Bouey, former governor of the Bank of Canada put it: "We did not abandon the monetary aggregates, they abandoned us."[4]

IF AT FIRST YOU DON'T SUCCEED: FINDING A NEW POLICY RULE . . .

As money targets lost their luster, focus has gradually shifted to targeting inflation. While central banks have less direct control over inflation than over money growth, by announcing inflation targets or goals, the central bank can lead the public to expect that any increase in inflationary pressures will be short-lived.

Over the past two decades, one by one the major central banks have adopted inflation targeting (table 8-1). In many cases the shift has been accompanied by new legislation increasing the independence of the central bank. These targeting regimes vary considerably in terms of how strict the rules are. At one extreme, the Bank of Japan's target is merely an informal summary of the range of views on price stability in the committee. At the other extreme, the Central Bank of Norway publishes the exact path of interest rates it thinks is consistent with achieving its inflation target; the governor of the Bank of England must write a letter to the Chancellor if inflation deviates by more than 1 percentage point from the target; and New Zealand law allows the governor to be dismissed if inflation performance is inadequate (although to my knowledge, no country has proposed capital punishment for violating the inflation target!).

The Fed is the only major central bank that has not adopted some form of inflation target. In part this is due to political resistance. However, the bigger reason is that Alan Greenspan was the last major central banker to advocate pure discretion in monetary policy. Indeed, he felt so strongly about this, the topic almost never came up for discussion at FOMC meetings. According to Bob Woodward, this came as a surprise to Janet Yellen when she became a Fed governor in the mid-1990s. Woodward writes, "Yellen was surprised that the Committee almost never talked about its overall strategy or its ultimate goals for acceptable rates of inflation. How can you operate if you do not know what your goal is?"[5]

Greenspan has said relatively little about his opposition to inflation targeting and it gets no mention in his memoirs. Perhaps the best, albeit indirect, statement of his views comes from a speech by Greenspan's close colleague at the Fed, Vice Chairman Donald Kohn.[6] Kohn has softened his views toward inflation targeting more recently, but back in 2003 Kohn argued, "if it ain't broke, don't fix it." The Fed had been successful in bringing down inflation without a target, so there seemed no need to establish one. Moreover, he thought an inflation target might compromise the Fed's dual man-

TABLE 8-1

Adoption of inflation targeting worldwide

Country	Date of adoption of inflation targeting	Current target*
New Zealand	March 1990	1–3
Chile	January 1991	2–4
Canada	February 1991	1–3
Israel	January 1992	1–3
United Kingdom	October 1992	2
Sweden	January 1993	2 (+/–1)
Peru	January 1994	2.5 (+/–1)
Australia	September 94	2–3
Czech Republic	January 1998	3 (+/–1)
Korea	January 1998	2.5–3.5
Poland	October 1998	2.5 (+/–1)
Mexico	January 1999	3 (+/–1)
Euro area	January 1999	< 2
Brazil	January 1999	4.5 (+/–2.5)
Colombia	September 1999	5 (+/–0.5)
Switzerland	January 2000	< 2
South Africa	February 2000	3–6
Thailand	April 2000	0–3.5
Iceland	March 2001	2.5
Norway	March 2001	2.5
Hungary	June 2001	3.5 (+/–1)
Philippines	January 2002	5–6

*In all cases in terms of CPI or variant thereof.

Sources: Adoption date: Mishkin and Schmidt-Hebbel (2001); current target; *Lehman Brothers Global Economics.*

date to foster both low inflation and high employment. Finally, adopting a target might open a Pandora's box, exposing the Fed to other changes in its structure or mandate.

I believe there are two other reasons for Greenspan's opposition to inflation targeting. First, adopting a target might have tied his hands, and Greenspan wanted to run policy unconstrained. Second, avoiding being pinned down with a specific inflation goal was part of the broader strategy of "constructive ambiguity." The Fed does not have precise control over inflation—recall the tugboat captain analogy from chapter 3—and if the target is missed the Fed would be open to public criticism. As Blinder and Reis argue, under the Greenspan standard, policy operated with "pure period-by-period discretion, with minimal strategic constraints of any kind, maximal tactical flexibility at all times, and not much in the way of explanation."[7]

THE GREENSPAN STANDARD
AND THE GOLD STANDARD

Frankly, I find Greenspan's views of policy discretion contradictory. On the one hand, in practice he embraced an almost purely discretionary approach. On the other hand, in his memoirs he notes that he "always harbored a nostalgia for the gold standard's inherent price stability."[8] Under the gold standard, central banks promised to exchange gold for their paper notes on demand. As a result, there was virtually no room for policy discretion: the growth in the money supply was determined simply by how much gold bullion was available. As Greenspan points out, the virtue of the gold standard is that "the average inflation rate under the gold and earlier commodity standards was essentially zero: at the height of the gold standard between 1870 and 1913 . . . the cost of living . . . rose a scant 0.2 percent per annum on average."[9] He also argues that the gold standard is unlikely to come back because it "does not readily accommodate the widely accepted current view of the appropriate functions of government—in particular the need for the government to provide a social safety net."[10] He worries that under our current fiat, or paper money, system there is a natural bias for inflation.[11]

   This raises a tough question: if the gold standard was a good way to impose disciplined monetary policy, why not impose other kinds of restraints? Targets for money supply growth, inflation, or nominal GDP growth can provide much the same discipline. As a disciplined mechanism for controlling inflation there is little difference between a low, rigid inflation target—where the central bank has almost no discretion—and the gold standard—where the central bank could change money supply only if the amount of gold increased.

The rigid rules of the gold standard made it impossible for central banks to fight recessions. Hence, while the inflation performance was impressive, the growth performance was awful. From 1870 to 1913 the U.S. economy was in recession 48 percent of the time—the average economic expansion lasted just 24 months and the average recession was 23 months. The straitjacket of the gold standard was by no means the only reason for this instability, but it was an important contributing factor. By contrast, over the last sixty years the economy has been in recession only 16 percent of the time, and during Greenspan's chairmanship there were only two short and shallow recessions. Greenspan seems to have an all-or-nothing approach to policy constraints, but surely there is an optimal middle ground between pure discretionary policy and the gold standard?

BERNANKE'S COMPROMISE

While Alan Greenspan quietly resisted the trend toward targeting, Princeton economics professor Ben Bernanke was busy building the case for targeting. He literally wrote the book on inflation targeting (and edited another), arguing that "Inflation targeting would be the better choice for monetary policy in both the United States and in Europe."[12] In his confirmation hearing for governor he said, "There is an area where, in fact, I have disagreed quite publicly with the chairman, and that is in the area of how best to achieve Federal Reserve transparency." He went on to explain how inflation targeting helps achieve that transparency.

There are two components to an inflation-targeting scheme. The first is obvious: the central bank must announce a specific numerical target or goal for inflation. Usually the target is given as a range for a specific measure of consumer price inflation. Second, and less obviously, most inflation-targeting central banks regularly publish forecasts for the economy and an explanation of how the central bank plans to achieve the target. This information often comes in the form of a regular inflation report that explains the forecast in detail. In some cases the central bank even announces the path for interest rates that it thinks will achieve the inflation goal.

Under Greenspan, and in Bernanke's first year and a half, the FOMC announced forecasts for the economy, but these were of rather dubious quality. Twice a year, each member of the committee would send in forecasts for four indicators—nominal GDP, real GDP, the unemployment rate, and inflation (recently, core PCE inflation). The range and central tendency of these forecasts would then be announced at the February and July Humphrey-Hawkins testimony. Although these forecasts got some attention in the markets, they seem to have played a secondary role in the policy process. At FOMC meetings, the forecasts of the board staff were presented in full detail, while the biannual forecasts of the FOMC members were rarely mentioned. Greenspan seemed to distance himself from the numbers.

There were often strange quirks in the numbers. For example, forecasts made in July of each year often did not seem to fully reflect what had happened earlier in the year.[13] I believe there are three reasons for the quirks. First, these projections were a mixture of goals and forecasts. To some extent the numbers were what FOMC members wanted to see, rather than what they expected. Second, some members had very little staff to crank out forecasts and they may have not run their forecasts through models or spreadsheets that would catch inconsistencies. Third, the forecast did not seem to play much of a role in the policy deliberations and so there was little incentive to sweat the details.

AN UGLY NEW ACRONYM

Initially, Bernanke favored a fairly rigid targeting scheme. In his 1999 book he and his coauthors argued that "the Humphrey-Hawkins legislation now in effect appears to be sufficiently broad and nonspecific to make new legislation unnecessary to implement the framework we have proposed here. Nevertheless, it would be desirable to modify the [law so that it] specifies that price stability is the overriding long-run objective of monetary policy, but also mandates attention to other important economic goals."[14] This would have aligned the Fed with most other inflation-targeting central banks.

As a Fed governor, Bernanke softened his views. This probably reflected a better understanding of the resistance he was likely to face from both other members of the FOMC and politicians. Table 8-2 shows where the FOMC stood before Bernanke became chairman. It suggests the seeds of a grand compromise: most members would be comfortable with some kind of target as long as the rules for achieving the target were flexible.

In a 2003 speech, Bernanke updated his view, laying out a targeting regime that looks more like a definition of price stability than

TABLE 8-2

Inflation-targeting scorecard

Against targeting/goals	For informal goals	For formal targets
Alan Greenspan *Chairman of the Board*	Edward Gramlich *Board member*	Ben S. Bernanke *Board member/Chairman, CEA*
Roger Ferguson *Vice-chairman of the Board*	Mark Olson *Board member*	Janet Yellen *San Francisco Fed*
Donald Kohn *Board member*	Richard Fisher *Dallas Fed*	Jeffrey Larcker *Richmond Fed*
Timothy Geithner *New York Fed*	Cathy Minehan *Boston Fed*	Anthony Santomero *Philadelphia Fed*
Michael Moskow *Chicago Fed*	Sandra Pianalto *Cleveland Fed*	Gary Stern *Minneapolis Fed*
		William Poole *St. Louis Fed*

Source: Federal Reserve, Bloomberg, and Lehman Brothers.

Note: Governor Susan Bies, Kansas's Thomas Hoenig, and Atlanta's Jack Guynn had not recently discussed their inflation targeting views.

a strict target. With this proposal he also introduced a new tongue twister to the economics literature: the optimal long-run inflation rate, or OLIR. No doubt this will rival the NAIRU (nonaccelerating inflation rate of unemployment) as one of the hardest-to-remember acronyms in economics. If you want to impress your friends, drop this double dose of economics jargon at your next dinner party: "Of course if the Fed is able to keep the unemployment rate near NAIRU they should be able to achieve their OLIR."

In fleshing out his new proposal, Bernanke was at pains to explain that he would not ignore the Fed's dual mandate for growth and inflation:

> To reassure those worried about possible loss of short-run flexibility, my proposal is that the FOMC announce its value for the OLIR to the public with the following provisos (not necessarily in these exact words):
>
> 1. The FOMC believes that the stated inflation rate is the one that best promotes its output, employment, and price stability goals in the long run. Hence, in the long run, the FOMC will try to guide the inflation rate toward the stated value and maintain it near that value on average over the business cycle.
>
> 2. However, the FOMC regards this inflation rate as a long-run objective only and sets no fixed time frame for reaching it. In particular, in deciding how quickly to move toward the long-run inflation objective, the FOMC will always take into account the implications for near-term economic and financial stability.
>
> As you can see, stating the OLIR with these provisos places no unwanted constraints on short-run monetary policy, leaving the Committee free to deal with current financial and cyclical conditions as the Committee sees fit. In this respect, the proposal is very similar to one recently advanced by Governor Gramlich (2003).[15]

HAVE YOUR CAKE AND EAT IT TOO

Bernanke believes that inflation targeting helps both ensure lower inflation and improve the growth performance of the economy. How is this possible? Because when the central bank adopts an inflation target, it encourages the public to expect continued low inflation. If workers and companies have confidence that the Fed will resist inflationary pressure, they may be slower to raise wages and prices when the economy is strong. This in turn would mean the Fed would not have to hit the brakes as hard—driving up the unemployment rate—to prevent inflation from accelerating. In other words, adopting an inflation target may have the added benefit of making it easier to maintain a low stable unemployment rate.

There is some evidence that the Fed's improved inflation credibility has already helped stabilize the unemployment rate. While Paul Volcker's initial war against inflation required very high interest rates and a surge in the unemployment rate, nothing nearly as drastic has been required to beat back inflation in the last two decades. Indeed there is evidence that consistently low inflation in many countries has changed the behavior of inflation. For example, models of U.S. inflation estimated with data before the mid-1980s show core inflation as tending to respond strongly to any sign of tightness in labor or commodity markets. By contrast, models estimated over the most recent period suggest that core inflation responds less to tightness in labor markets, and does not rise at all in response to oil prices.[16]

THE PRINCETON BACKDOOR PLAY

With his strong commitment to targeting, it is not surprising that one of Bernanke's first actions as Fed chairman was to form a subcommittee to explore changes in the ways the Fed communicates. More than a year and a half later, on November 14, 2007, the Fed's new communications strategy was announced. The FOMC decided to report its forecasts four times a year instead of twice a year, with the forecasts extending out three years instead of two. Each member makes the forecasts based on his or her own assumptions about appropriate monetary policy. The new forecasts are presented at the FOMC meeting, encouraging members to own their forecasts.

For many economists, the new plan seemed like a very small move after such long deliberations. The reason for releasing forecasts is to arm the public with a better understanding of what is driving Fed policy and how policy might change if circumstances change. However, these forecasts provide very little guidance. Each member makes his or her own assumptions about the variables driving the forecast: fiscal policy, oil prices, asset prices, and, most important, the appropriate monetary policy. However, if we don't know what the underlying assumptions are, we have no way to know how the Fed will react if the economy is weaker or stronger than expected. For example, suppose the public is worried about recession, but the Fed forecasts healthy growth. Does that mean the Fed thinks the economy is fine and doesn't need any help, or does it mean the Fed is assuming big rate cuts will prevent the recession?

On the surface, Bernanke seems to have postponed his push for a formal inflation target; in reality, the new communication process seems to be a way for the FOMC to reveal its inflation target without calling it one. Here's how: in making a forecast, each FOMC member is supposed to assume *appropriate monetary policy*. For a modern central banker, appropriate monetary policy is policy that steers inflation (and unemployment) to acceptable levels over the longer term. At the time of Bernanke's announcement, the economy was not particularly out of equilibrium—for example, the unemployment rate was in the neighborhood of NAIRU and core inflation was in, or near, the FOMC's comfort zone. Three years is plenty of time for appropriate monetary policy to achieve appropriate inflation. In other words, in forecasting three years ahead, FOMC members were revealing their preferred inflation targets.

As a longtime Princeton professor, Bernanke must have been familiar with the backdoor play, a way for a smaller, slower basketball team (like Princeton) to score against a bigger, faster team (like

Georgetown). In a backdoor play, a player runs toward the passer, then abruptly reverses course and cuts to the basket. With a well-timed pass, the player can make a lay-up. Whether intentional or not, Bernanke has introduced what looks like an improved forecast, but is really a backdoor way to reveal the level of inflation acceptable to the FOMC. The results show very little disagreement on the committee: the most hawkish member favored a 1.5 percent target and the most dovish favored a 2.0 percent target. The central tendency range, excluding the three lowest and three highest targets, was 1.6 to 1.9 percent (figure 8-2).[17]

Just in case anyone did not get the message, Fed Governor Frederic Mishkin laid out the logic in a speech in November 2007:

> The projections for both overall and core inflation at the three-year horizon (which is currently 2010) fall in the range of 1.5 percent to 2.0 percent; the central tendency of these projections is 1.6 percent to 1.9 percent . . . Each FOMC participant's projection is made under the assumption of "appropriate" monetary policy—that is, the path of policy calibrated to achieve outcomes for economic activity and inflation that are most consistent with our dual objectives of

FIGURE 8-2

FOMC forecasts of core PCE inflation

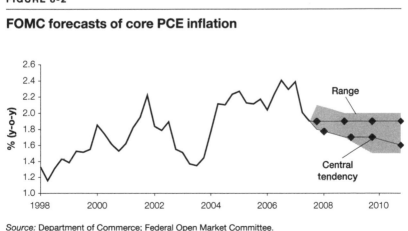

Source: Department of Commerce; Federal Open Market Committee.

price stability and maximum employment. For that reason, the longer-run inflation projections provide information about each FOMC participant's assessment of the inflation rate that best promotes those dual objectives—a rate that I will refer to as the "mandate-consistent inflation rate."[18]

Thus, in an attempt to avoid a "politically incorrect" phrase like "inflation target," we now have not only the optimal long-run inflation rate (OLIR) but the mandate-consistent inflation rate (MCIR). All I can say is: SOS.

With the inflation goals of the FOMC members revealed, the FOMC can now turn to making the forecasts useful. The most obvious step would be to impose a consistent assumption for monetary policy. The easiest approach is for each FOMC member to make their growth and inflation forecast assuming the funds rate follows what the futures market is expecting. In the Fed funds futures market investors make bets about whether the Fed will lower or raise the funds rate in the coming months. By explicitly tying the economic forecasts to the market expectations for the Fed, the FOMC growth and inflation forecasts become much more informative. If growth or inflation were higher than the Fed expected, the public could then infer that the Fed would push rates up faster than the markets had been expecting. It would be another small step toward a modern central bank communication strategy.

DON'T ASK, DON'T TELL

A move to an announced "soft" inflation target or goal is long overdue. In recent years the targeting debate has started to take on an Alice in Wonderland quality. While some members of Congress strongly oppose inflation targeting, and the debate inside the Fed rages on, in reality, the Fed has had a soft target for many years. Starting in 2006 the press regularly refers to Bernanke's 1 to 2 percent comfort zone for core PCE inflation. The Fed has been acting as though such a range exists: core PCE inflation was between 1 and 2 percent continuously from March 1996 to April 2004, averaging 1.6 percent. When inflation threatened to drop below that zone, Fed officials promised aggressive action if necessary, and when it has drifted above that range in 2006, the FOMC made clear its bias to tighten policy (until the capital markets crisis shifted the Fed's focus).

Even more telling, the FOMC agreed to a "secret" internal target in 1996. At the July 1996 FOMC meeting, after a long discussion of the Fed's inflation goals, Alan Greenspan announced, "We have now agreed on 2 percent [as a target for CPI inflation]."[19] Allowing for measurement differences at the time, this is equivalent to a target of 1.5 percent for the PCE deflator—and that happens to be exactly the midpoint of the range Bernanke proposed as a Fed governor. Of course, back in 1996 the super-secretive Greenspan went on to warn his committee: "I will tell you that if the 2 percent inflation figure gets out of this room, it is going to create more problems for us than I think any of you might anticipate."[20] For a few green-eyeshade-wearing economists with the fortitude to read the Fed's transcripts, the Greenspan Fed had an inflation "target" for more than a decade.

SEVENTEEN ECONOMISTS, THIRTY-FOUR OPINIONS

Why did it take Bernanke so long to achieve such a small step? One problem is that longer-term strategy planning keeps getting interrupted by a very challenging near-term policy environment. Bernanke's more democratic style also slows the process. He does not want to ram a decision through the committee; rather, he wants a strong consensus. Another problem is the large size of the FOMC. There are nineteen members (although two seats were empty during Bernanke's first two years) and while normally only twelve vote at any given meeting, a strategic decision like establishing inflation targets requires the support of the whole committee. Bernanke may be feeling a bit like President Harry Truman, who once joked that he wished he had a "one-armed economist" so he could quit getting two views on every issue.

A final reason for the slow progress is the risk of political backlash. Pushing through a target that is later overturned by Congress does not accomplish anything. Barney Frank, the powerful chairman of the House Financial Services Committee, has said it would be a "terrible mistake" to adopt an inflation target. He argues that the Fed has a "statutory mandate for stable prices and low unemployment. If you target one of them and not the other, it seems to me that will inevitably be favored."[21]

Fed officials and most macroeconomists disagree with Mr. Frank's economics, but explaining the modern Phillips Curve to noneconomists is not easy. The problem with Frank's view is that it implicitly assumes a model of the economy that has long been abandoned by most economists, who no longer believe in the idea of a permanent stable trade-off between unemployment and inflation. In the modern Phillips Curve, if the Fed targets the unemployment rate it is almost certain to end up with an unstable economy. If it picks too low a target, and attempts to stick to it, the result will be an upward spiral in inflation. Equally ominous, if the Fed adopts too high a target, spiraling deflation might ensue.

All of this highlights the nightmare scenario for the Fed: could it, in its attempt to establish an inflation target, be saddled with an unworkable unemployment rate target? One could imagine the Congressional hearing:

> **Congressman:** Mr. Bernanke, what would be a sensible target for the unemployment rate that would achieve acceptable rates of inflation?
>
> **Bernanke:** As I've said before, setting such a target would be quite dangerous, but recent research suggests the inflation neutral unemployment rate is in the neighborhood of 5 percent. Of course, there is considerable uncertainty about the exact value . . .

Congressman: You are aware that a 5 percent unemployment rate translates in human terms to almost 8 million Americans out of work. Does it make sense to adopt a policy that dooms such a large group to unemployment? Keep in mind that the job losses will hit the most vulnerable parts of the economy hardest—for example, if the overall unemployment rate is 5 percent, that could mean 9 percent for African Americans and 30 percent for African American teenagers. Can't we do better? Why not spare millions of workers the pain of unemployment with a 4 percent target? I for one would be prepared to back legislation for a 2 percent inflation target and a 4 percent target for the unemployment rate.

Bernanke: Sir, I'd like to withdraw my suggestion that we target anything.

Such a scenario is unlikely, but it is worth remembering that this is effectively what happened in the 1960s, before economists had discovered the instability of the Phillips Curve. At the time it was widely agreed that 4 percent was an acceptable goal for the unemployment rate. With inflation accelerating from below 2 percent at the start of the decade to 6 percent, at the end it became clear, in hindsight, that the goal was not achievable. After a long period of procrastination and soul-searching, the inflation genie was not put back in the bottle until more than a decade later.

THE THIRTY YEARS WAR

It is hard to overstate the importance of an inflation target to Bernanke. In several speeches he has noted that is the one area of substantive difference between him and Greenspan. Inflation targeting would complete the nearly thirty-year war against inflation started by Paul Volcker in 1979. Alan Greenspan continued to drive inflation lower: for the last decade of his chairmanship, core PCE inflation averaged 1.7 percent. However, in Bernanke's mind, the war will not be truly over until the new borders have been established on paper. He knows that for every strong inflation fighter—a Volcker or a Greenspan—there is a weak chairman—a Burns or a Miller. Hence the Fed needs to codify its goals. I would imagine that Bernanke probably views the adoption of a target as the defining event of his chairmanship.

9

Depression Obsession

How the Great Depression Informs Bernanke's Thinking

Modern central banking is defined by the two big policy mistakes of the last century: the Great Depression of the 1930s, and the Great Inflation of the 1970s.[1] While Bernanke's views have been molded by both events, his academic research shows a particular interest in the Great Depression. In his book on the Depression, he wrote, "I guess I am a Great Depression buff, the way some people are Civil War buffs."[2]

Data from the 1930s underscores why Bernanke views the Depression as such a crucial event in economic history. From 1929 to 1933 the level of U.S. GDP collapsed, falling by an astonishing 30 percent. Industrial production fell even faster: by 1933 it was roughly half the level of just four years earlier. The unemployment rate rose to 25 percent (figure 9-1). There was an extended period of deflation: the price level fell by 25 percent (figure 9-2). As I will show, deflation undercuts the vitality of the economy and makes it hard to operate monetary policy. Clearly, if we want to understand

FIGURE 9-1

Unemployment rate during the Great Depression

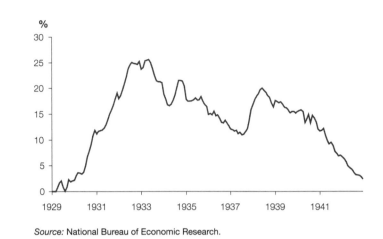

Source: National Bureau of Economic Research.

FIGURE 9-2

The price level during the Great Depression

Source: National Bureau of Economic Research.

economic downturns, a good place to start is with the worst economic collapse in modern times.

Bernanke's Depression studies are not just an area of academic
interest: they help inform his current policy outlook. They explain
why he judges that some inflation—an inflation target of 1 to 2 per-

cent—is a good thing. That 1 percent lower limit is a very important cushion against deflation. Bernanke's studies have also motivated his aggressive criticism of Japan's tepid response to its recent decade of deflation. And they also explain why in 2002 and 2003 he was the Fed's point person in explaining how the Fed might respond if deflation were to emerge in the United States. Unfortunately, this attempt to teach the public about deflation and depression has also contributed to a widespread—and completely wrong—view that Bernanke is an anti-inflation dove. The whole idea of inflation targeting is to be a hawk—in the sense of acting aggressively—when either boundary is violated.

EXTREME TIMES CALL FOR
EXTREME MEASURES

It came as a bit of a shock in 2002 and 2003 when, after battling inflation for twenty-five years, Fed officials started to talk about the risk of inflation getting too low. In November 2002, in a speech titled "Making Sure 'It' Doesn't Happen Here," Bernanke led the charge, arguing that the "chance of significant deflation in the United States . . . is extremely small," but the costs are so high that it is crucial to have a battle plan for fighting deflation.[3]

What is deflation and why worry about it? In ordinary times some prices are rising and others are falling, but in a *"deflation"* there is a broad-based drop in prices. As Bernanke defined it, "Deflation is in almost all cases a side effect of a collapse of aggregate demand—a drop in spending so severe that producers must continually cut prices in order to find buyers. Likewise, the economic effects of a deflationary episode are, for the most part, similar to those of any other sharp decline in aggregate spending—namely, recession, rising unemployment, and financial stress."[4]

Deflation creates three additional problems on top of the normal stress of a recession. First, because interest rates cannot go below zero, it can cause real borrowing costs to rise. To illustrate this, Bernanke takes the extreme case of the 10 percent deflation during part of the Great Depression: "[S]omeone who borrows for a year at a nominal interest rate of zero actually faces a 10 percent real cost of funds, as the loan must be repaid in dollars whose purchasing power is 10 percent greater than that of the dollars borrowed originally. In a period of sufficiently severe deflation, the real cost of borrowing becomes prohibitive. Capital investment, purchases of new homes, and other types of spending decline accordingly, worsening the economic downturn."[5]

Second, as tough as deflation is for new borrowers, it is even tougher on people who borrowed at normal interest rates before deflation began. As Bernanke notes, "Even if debtors are able to refinance their existing obligations at low nominal interest rates, with prices falling they must still repay the principal in dollars of increasing (perhaps rapidly increasing) real value." Again, Bernanke points to the lessons of the Great Depression, which caused "massive financial problems, including defaults, bankruptcies, and bank failures . . . in America's worst encounter with deflation."[6]

The third challenge from deflation is that it undercuts monetary policy. As I have discussed, the Fed's main tool for battling recession is to cut the federal funds rate. However, once the funds rate reaches zero, the Fed's conventional policy ammunition is gone. Once the Fed hits the zero boundary, the worse deflation gets, and the higher the real cost of borrowing. Hitting the zero boundary may also be bad for consumer and business confidence if the public begins to believe the Fed is out of ammunition.

A MONETARY MECHANISM GONE WRONG

Deflation was an important part of the economic dysfunction during the Great Depression. The blame for the massive failures of the Depression is spread widely. Bernanke points to Fed policy, the gold standard, and rigid labor markets.

Bernanke followed in the footsteps of Milton Friedman, whose book, *A Monetary History of the United States*, coauthored with Anna Schwartz, revolutionized understanding of the Great Depression.[7]

In a 2002 speech honoring Milton Friedman's ninetieth birthday, Bernanke concluded: "Let me end my talk by abusing slightly my status as an official representative of the Federal Reserve. I would like to say to Milton and Anna: Regarding the Great Depression. You're right, we did it. We're very sorry. But thanks to you, we won't do it again."[8]

For Bernanke, the starting point for the Depression was the Federal Reserve's significant monetary tightening in the spring of 1928. The Fed responded to concern about speculation on Wall Street: too much credit was flowing into "speculative" rather than "productive" uses. The next mistake is that the Fed did nothing to stem the massive wave of bank failures in the early 1930s: "Fed officials appeared to subscribe to Treasury Secretary Andrew Mellon's infamous 'liquidationist' thesis, thus weeding out 'weak' banks was a harsh but necessary prerequisite to the recovery of the banking system, in the belief that they were 'purging' rottenness out of the financial system." The third mistake was a rigid adherence to the gold standard that forced the Fed to drain liquidity from the system to stop the outflow of gold.[9]

GOLD OR PYRITE?

In his memoirs, Alan Greenspan writes of "nostalgia for the gold standard's inherent price stability."[10] Bernanke seems less nostalgic: he mainly associates the gold standard with its role in the Depression. Under the gold standard, governments agreed to redeem their currency upon demand for a designated amount of gold. Under this rigid system, central banks could increase the amount of liquidity in the economy only if there was an increase in the supply of gold. If there was hoarding of gold—as in the 1930s—central banks were forced to reduce the supply of money. Bernanke writes, "There is now overwhelming evidence that the main factor depressing aggregate demand was a worldwide contraction in world money supplies." The proof of the pudding is the behavior of economies when the gold standard was removed (figure 9-3): "When intense downward

FIGURE 9-3

**Industrial production in countries with and without
the gold standard**

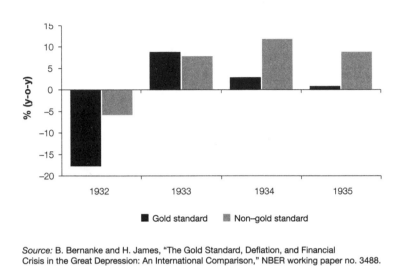

Source: B. Bernanke and H. James, "The Gold Standard, Deflation, and Financial
Crisis in the Great Depression: An International Comparison," NBER working paper no. 3488.

pressures on aggregate demand were removed (for example, through devaluation of an exchange rate or the abandonment of the gold standard), many countries experienced fairly rapid recoveries in output and employment."[11]

NOMINAL RIGIDITIES

The third major cause of the Depression was wage rigidity. During periods of extreme economic weakness firms face a choice of cutting wages or workers. For example, during the Depression my own grandfather kept his dairy workers employed for several years using a form of wage cuts—workers were paid in dairy products. However, this was not the norm. Wages did not fall by nearly enough to bring labor markets back into equilibrium. Bernanke writes, "The adjustment of nominal wages in response to declines in aggregate demand during the 1930s was surprisingly slow and incomplete."

As prices fell, nominal wages stayed unchanged: hence, real wages rose in a very low aggregate demand environment. "The econometric evidence offers reasonably strong support for the hypothesis that slowly adjusting nominal wages helped propagate monetary shocks in the Depression." Bernanke observes, ". . . there existed a strong inverse relationship (across countries as well as over time) between output and real wages."[12]

Bernanke's study of the Depression is not stale textbook stuff. It suggests several lessons for today. First, it is important to not stick to rigid doctrines. Otherwise, as he says, "Institutions which evolve and perform well in normal times may become counterproductive during periods when exogenous shocks or policy mistakes drive the economy off course."[13] Second, Bernanke has no sympathy for the idea of liquidating rot from the system. In the current environment, that means he would not favor purging the economy of imbalances—slowing growth purely for the sake of reducing the trade deficit, raising interest rates to restore personal saving rates, or punishing investors for buying subprime mortgages. The Fed does not want to be bailing out the markets, but neither does it want to allow the economy to collapse for the sake of policy purity. Third, his work suggests that as long as there are "nominal rigidities" in the economy, deflation is to be avoided through aggressive preemptive action. Inflation targets need a lower bound that is above zero.

JAPAN'S LOST DECADE

For Bernanke, history and present reality intersected when it came to Japan's recent decade of deflation (figure 9-4). From 1986 to 1990 a severe bubble in the Japanese stock and property markets expanded and then popped, triggering more than a decade of weak growth and repeated recessions. With the economic weakness came a mild deflation, with the general price level falling modestly from the mid-1990s.

As a Fed governor, Bernanke went to Tokyo in May 2003 to present "Some Thoughts on Monetary Policy in Japan." Despite the

FIGURE 9-4

The Japanese consumer price index

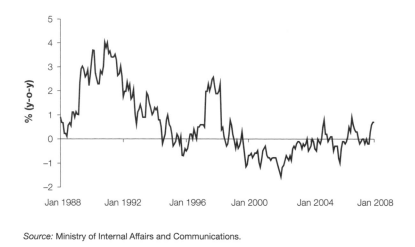

Source: Ministry of Internal Affairs and Communications.

innocuous title, the speech was—by central banker standards—a radical call to arms. Here was nothing less than an official of the Federal Reserve talking about the "frustratingly slow pace of change in Japan," and urging Japanese economists to "speak out and present clear, persuasive arguments that will help guide the policy debate and urge leaders to effective action."[14] Not surprisingly, Bernanke's speech was not welcomed by Japanese policy makers, including many of his counterparts at Japan's central bank, the Bank of Japan (BOJ).

Why incur the wrath of the BOJ? Like many western economists, Bernanke was frustrated with Japan's tentative approach in their war against deflation. Bernanke told a skeptical audience that it was the central banks' duty not only to end deflation but also to create higher-than-normal inflation to offset the drop in wages and prices of the recent period. Specifically, he recommended a two-part strategy (figure 9-5). First, there should be a "reflationary phase": the BOJ should push up inflation to make up for the previous five years of falling prices. Then, once the price declines had been reversed, the BOJ should maintain inflation of at least 1 percent in the years ahead.

FIGURE 9-5

Bernanke's price level advice to Japan

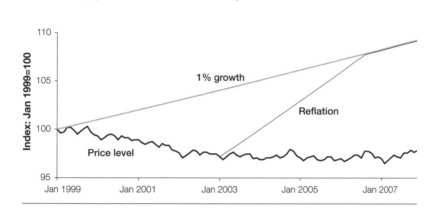

In Bernanke's mind, Japan was repeating the policy errors of the Great Depression. Long-term borrowers took out loans in Japan on the assumption that wages and prices would rise over time—hence, as in most countries, there was an inflation premium included in the interest rate. When prices fell, this created "intense pressure on debtors and the financial system in general . . . weakening the banking system and depressing investment spending."[15] Here Bernanke's knowledge of the Great Depression came in handy: "Reflation—that is, a period of inflation above the long-run preferred rate in order to restore the earlier price level—proved highly beneficial following the deflations of the 1930s in both Japan and the United States. Finance Minister Korekiyo Takahashi brilliantly rescued Japan from the Great Depression through reflationary policies in the early 1930s, while President Franklin D. Roosevelt's reflationary monetary and banking policies did the same for the United States in 1933 and subsequent years."[16]

By 1995 the BOJ had already reduced its interest rate to zero, so the conventional limits of monetary policy had been reached. Bernanke suggested a further radical step: enact a "tax cut for households and businesses that is explicitly coupled with incremental BOJ purchases of government debt—so that the tax cut is in effect financed by money creation."[17]

For Bernanke, the key to Japan's deflationary problem lay in recognizing that:

> The role of a central bank is different in inflationary and deflationary environments. In the face of inflation, which is often associated with excessive monetization of government debt, the virtue of an independent central bank is its ability to say "no" to the government. With protracted deflation, however, excessive money creation is unlikely to be the problem, and a more cooperative stance on the part of the central bank may be called for. Under the current circumstances, greater cooperation for a time between the Bank of Japan and the fiscal authorities is in no way inconsistent with the independence of the central bank, any more than cooperation between two independent nations in pursuit of a common objective is inconsistent with the principle of national sovereignty.[18]

While Bernanke is unlikely to speak out in his new position as Fed chairman, the BOJ has not followed his advice. Land and stock prices have started to inch up, but remain well below normal levels, let alone their peak levels (figure 9-6). Consumer prices have stabi-

FIGURE 9-6

Mount Fuji: Land prices in Japan

Source: Japan Real Estate Institute.

lized, but the recovery has been very slow. Yet the BOJ has started slowly to hike interest rates. It has also adopted an informal inflation target, but it is the lowest of any targeting nation in the world—between zero and 2 percent. I believe Japan should be following Bernanke's reflationary advice. A country that has recently experienced deflation is highly susceptible to falling back into deflation, because consumers and businesses still have a deflation psychology, a reflexive tendency to pull back on spending at the first sign of economic weakness. Japan needs a period of sustained above-target inflation to vanquish this psychology.

TOO CLOSE FOR COMFORT

In 2002 and 2003, with talk that the United States could mimic Japan, Bernanke took up the public relations challenge, announcing that "the chance of significant deflation in the United States in the foreseeable future is extremely small." Bernanke argued that a central bank can preempt deflation in three ways. "First, the Fed should try to preserve a buffer zone for the inflation rate, that is, during normal times it should not try to push inflation down all the way to zero." "Second, the Fed should take most seriously—as of course it does—its responsibility to ensure financial stability in the economy." Third, "as suggested by a number of studies, when inflation is already low and the fundamentals of the economy suddenly deteriorate, the central bank should act more preemptively and more aggressively than usual in cutting rates."[19]

But what if deflation comes on suddenly and all attempts to stop it fail? Fear not. While deflation is a challenge to policy makers, even with a zero funds rate, a central bank has most definitely not run out of ammunition. For Bernanke, and most economists, the idea that a central bank is helpless in the face of deflation makes no sense. In a fiat money system (that is, where money is simply printed with no gold or other backing) money costs virtually nothing to create, so the central bank can simply print and distribute money until inflation occurs.

Specifically, Bernanke lays out how the Fed can escalate its war against deflation.

Step one: push the funds rate to zero.

Step two: drive down long-term Treasury interest rates by either promising to keep short rates low for a number of years or commit to make unlimited purchases of Treasury bonds until their interest rate falls.

Step three: push down interest rates on private securities by buying them up as well.

Step four: intervene aggressively in the foreign exchange market to weaken the dollar and raise the price of imports.

Step five: have a coordinated easing of both monetary and fiscal policy, with, for example, a cut in taxes financed by issuing money so there is no increase in government debt.

Bernanke concluded: "a money-financed tax cut is essentially equivalent to Milton Friedman's famous 'helicopter drop' of money."[20]

STREET FIGHTING MAN

In sum, Bernanke believes the war on deflation is like a street fight: it will always be won as long as you are willing to keep adopting increasingly radical steps to vanquish your opponent. Does this mean he is "Helicopter Ben" after all, willing to air-drop cash until inflation runs out of control. No, in Bernanke's mind, radical policy easing is only acceptable if there is a serious risk of economic collapse due to deflation, a collapse in the financial sector, or some other major downside shock. Moreover, as with much of the confusion about Bernanke, this misnomer comes partly from confusing Bernanke and Greenspan's approach to communication. One always had to read between Greenspan's lines: if he talked about a "remote risk" he usually meant a "real risk." When Bernanke talks about a remote risk that is exactly what he means. What he had in mind was a contingency plan that, even in the very low inflation period of 2002 to 2003, was never close to being implemented.

10

Glasnost

Democracy Comes to the Fed

Most of the discussion in this book has focused on the substance of policy under Bernanke, but style also matters. In this chapter I explore how the internal workings of the Fed changed under Bernanke. Specifically, I'll look at how the passing of the mantle from a data junkie to a former academic has changed the economic and policy discussion within the Fed. I also look at the implications of having a less dominant chairman.

REARRANGING THE ECONOMICS TOOLKIT

Over the years a widening gap has developed between academic research and what business economists and policy makers do. Academic research has become very high tech, and the focus has shifted to increasingly narrow questions that can be addressed only with complicated math and statistics. By contrast, business and policy economics remains decidedly low tech: most of the interesting questions need to be answered quickly and are not easily modeled. Hence, even though most top graduate students go into academia, when the Bush administration began looking for Greenspan's replacement, the list of qualified academics was short.

Greenspan was famous for his ability to gather and analyze a wide range of facts and figures. When Bernanke's candidacy for Fed chairman was announced, a common concern was that the Fed would be losing the strong business economics skills of which Greenspan was a master. For example, during the trial balloon phase of finding a new chairman, a *Wall Street Journal* op-ed piece said the White House was "very concerned that whoever they get not only has understanding of monetary policy, but experience working with financial markets and the ability to use business and market contacts to get ahead of the statistical data."[1] Bernanke certainly does not fit this description. Other than a very brief stint at the Council of Economic Advisers and a few years as a Fed governor, Bernanke spent his entire career in academia. Unlike Greenspan, who spent most of his career as an economic consultant, Bernanke entered the job with very little experience in the nitty-gritty of economic forecasting.

THE ART AND SCIENCE
OF ECONOMIC FORECASTING

The good news is that Bernanke was well aware of his shortcomings, and as a Fed governor he immediately set about correcting them. In 2005, in a speech on "The Transition from Academic to Policymaker," Bernanke made clear that he understood exactly what he was up against. He admits, "A part of monetary policymaking for which my background left me imperfectly prepared is what central bankers call 'current analysis.'"[2]

This speech is worth quoting at length because it illustrates his acceptance of a broad array of tools in economic forecasting. Bernanke starts by noting the importance of having a strong academic foundation for thinking about the economy:

I have found the knowledge and habits of thinking developed in my academic days to be quite useful. The models and forecasting methods used by the Federal Reserve staff, for example, draw heavily on decades of academic research and thus feel comfortably familiar. Academic research (by which I mean to include technical research done in central banks and other non-academic institutions) also bears directly on many strategic aspects of monetary policymaking. For example, the Federal Open Market Committee has recently been engaged in developing its communications strategy, a topic which I believe to be of vital importance and on which I have spoken on numerous occasions. My thinking on this and numerous other aspects of monetary policy is heavily influenced by contemporary research in monetary economics, as can be seen by the footnotes and citations in my speeches.

However, Bernanke is not a dewy-eyed academic. He writes:

One of the biggest practical challenges of making monetary policy—and a prerequisite for any serious forecasting exercise—is getting an accurate assessment of the current economic situation. Doing this well requires a deep knowledge of the data mixed with a goodly dose of economic theory and economic judgment. Members of the Board staff continuously analyze the arriving data to learn what they can about the level and composition of economic activity, inflation, and other key aggregates. At the most mechanical level, this exercise requires a detailed understanding of how the U.S. statistical agencies use the information in current data releases to estimate economic aggregates—how the components of retail sales are linked to estimates of personal consumption, for example. But often the linkages between data releases and the key economic aggregates are not so straightforward . . . A certain amount of uncertainty in the estimates is unavoidable, of course; indeed, identifying the sources of uncertainty is an important part of the analysis. However, the requirements of internal consistency—production must always equal sales plus inventory investment, for example—provide numerous cross-checks and substantial discipline on this process.

More generally, all of us involved in the monetary policy process must try to synthesize a range of disparate information, including official data, anecdotes, and qualitative developments, to construct a "story" about how the economy is evolving: What forces are determining economic activity now, and what do they portend for the future? Chairman Greenspan is, of course, a master of current analysis and near-term forecasting, and many members of the National Association for Business Economics have finely honed these skills as well. Current analysis is not taught in graduate school, probably for good reason; it seems more amenable to on-the-job training. It is, nevertheless, an intellectually challenging activity—analogous, it seems to me, to the efforts of a detective to reconstruct a sequence of events from a range of diverse and subtle clues—and I have enjoyed the opportunity to become more proficient at it.[3]

This passage reveals several aspects of Bernanke's approach. First, he recognizes both the art and science of economic forecasting. A good forecaster must weave together models, storytelling, and an understanding of the details of the data. Second, the chair need not figure it all out all alone. No economic forecasting institution in the United States has anything close to the Fed's access to anecdotal information. There is a huge talented staff at the board of governors and at each of the Reserve Banks. Economists at the twelve regional Reserve Banks gather a massive amount of industry data eight times a year, compiling it into the so-called "Beige Book." The quarterly Senior Loan Officer survey takes the pulse of the banking system four times a year. The Open Market Desk at the Federal Reserve Bank of New York is in constant contact with financial markets. An effective chairman does not need to be personally involved in this data collection effort; what's needed is a strong staff and an ability to sort through and judge the staff's analyses.

There is no substitute for experience in forecasting and the Fed has lost an extremely experienced forecaster with Greenspan's retirement. However, I prefer Bernanke's balanced approach to forecasting to Greenspan's heavy reliance on anecdotal evidence and gut feeling. Moreover, it is worth recalling that Greenspan also had some gaps in his experience when he took over the Fed chairmanship. As Bob Woodward writes, "Greenspan liked the mechanical, analytical work of basic business economics—inventories, arithmetic, physical reality. Monetary policy, the setting of interest rates, was far more complex."[4] Thus while Greenspan brought strong business economics skills, he did not have the deep understanding of the history and theory of monetary policy that Bernanke has. Over time Greenspan seemed to get a bit overconfident in his "gut feeling" approach to forecasting. Greenspan's biggest call as a forecaster was his early understanding of the surge in labor productivity in the late 1990s. After that success he seemed to rely less on the forecasts and research of the Fed staff. By contrast, Bernanke seems at pains to anchor his thinking in the research of others. Like a guess hitter in baseball, Greenspan's approach belted out some home runs, but he had some strikeouts as well. Bernanke's doubles are less impressive, but could prove as productive.

Bernanke's reaction to the credit crunch of 2007 shows his flexibility in forecasting. During financial crises, a good economic forecaster shifts focus away from models and zeros in on both timely economic indicators and on the complex linkages between capital markets and the economy. Thus, at the height of market turmoil in August 2007 Bernanke argued:

> In light of recent financial developments, economic data bearing on past months or quarters may be less useful than usual for our forecasts of economic activity and inflation. Consequently, we will pay particularly close attention to the timeliest indicators, as well as information gleaned from our business and banking contacts around the country.

Inevitably, the uncertainty surrounding the outlook will be greater than normal, presenting a challenge to policymakers to manage the risks to their growth and price stability objectives. The Committee continues to monitor the situation and will act as needed to limit the adverse effects on the broader economy that may arise from the disruptions in financial markets.[5]

Bernanke's approach has changed the focus of Fed watchers. Under Greenspan the markets tended to obsess around the latest hot indicator—purchasing managers indexes, the "P star" inflation predictor (a model linking prices to money growth), freight car loadings (a supposed early indicator of shifts in economic activity), measures of home equity extraction, and so forth. While these indicators still matter, under Bernanke key research papers out of the policy community may attract similar attention. These days, I'm keeping a close eye not only on Bernanke's own research but on the working papers coming out of the Federal Reserve Board and the Reserve Banks.

AN ORCHESTRA WITHOUT THE MAESTRO

Perhaps the biggest change in style is the now well-advertised return to a more democratic committee at the Fed. Blinder and Reis note that Greenspan "has been on the job so long, and has been so dominant and successful, that few Americans any longer draw any distinction between 'Alan Greenspan' and 'the Federal Reserve'. . . Furthermore, this is not far from the truth."[6] One of the most visible manifestations of this dominance is that FOMC members rarely vote against the chairman at FOMC meetings. Keep in mind that, excluding the chairman, there are usually between ten and twelve voting members on the FOMC and there are at least eight votes per year, implying an average of close to one hundred opportunities to dissent per year. During Greenspan's tenure, actual annual dissents fell from a high of eleven in the late 1980s to almost none in his last seven years.[7]

The 1994 tightening cycle is a dramatic example of Greenspan's ability to dominate his committee at key decision points.[8] By the beginning of 1994, the Fed had been on hold, with an unusually low 3 percent funds rate, for seventeen straight months. Worried about an overheating economy, the committee was itching to hike rates. Chairman Greenspan came into the February meeting expecting the debate to be about whether to adopt a bias to tighten or to raise rates 25 basis points. He said, "I would put on the table my preference that at this meeting we move up 25 basis points. But if that is not the view of the Committee, I would urge that we at least go asymmetric." However, the committee was in a hawkish mood. Of the nine voters on the committee other than Greenspan, six expressed a clear preference for a 50-basis-point policy move. Ultimately, in a tour de force, Greenspan not only got a majority to vote for 25 basis points, but he convinced every member to "accept" a 25-basis-point hike.

How did he pull this off? He put his personal reputation on the line: "I've been in the economic forecasting business since 1948 . . . and I'm telling you I have this pain in my stomach which I have been very successful in alluding to. I am telling you . . . this is not the time to do this."[9] He managed the discussion by calling on allies, turning to New York Fed President William McDonough for support. He used his position as chairman, countering individually each argument for the 50-basis-point hike. He framed the voting choice, suggesting that the FOMC members were all in agreement to hike rates. He appealed to the higher principles of the group: "It is a very potent message out in the various communities with which we deal if we stand together."[10] (A side note: Greenspan was probably wrong to restrain the committee, since the Fed ended up hiking rates many more times that year.)

In his book, former governor Laurence Meyer describes Greenspan's attempts to curb public statements by FOMC members:

> "At one of our FOMC meetings, the Chairman said he thought too much 'chatter' was going on between FOMC meetings."

> "The Chairman preferred Committee members to talk as little as possible about the outlook and monetary policy."

"At one meeting, the Chairman asked the Committee how it might discipline itself."

"The Chairman encouraged [the idea that the] head of public affairs at the Board develop guidelines that specified what Committee members should and should not talk about."[11]

Meyer goes on to note his own resistance to strict rules around public speaking, but he also suggests that he accepted the idea that he was to try to avoid moving the markets. Given the chairman's prestige, this pressure to conform must have had a chilling effect on the committee's public comments.

SAFETY IN NUMBERS

When Bernanke stepped into the Fed chairmanship, he deliberately set about redistributing power away from himself and to his committee. As Vincent Reinhart, former secretary of the FOMC, points out, "Eschewing the power and trappings of authority is not an everyday occurance in Washington, DC."[12] Back in 2000 Bernanke gave a strong hint of how he would operate as Fed chairman. In an op-ed piece coauthored with Frederic Mishkin and Adam Posen, Bernanke argued that adopting an inflation target would depersonalize the Fed: "Adoption of inflation targeting by the Federal Reserve would . . . transform the commitment to price stability—which has served us so well under Mr. Greenspan and his predecessor, Paul Volcker—from a personal preference of the chairman into an official policy. By depersonalizing and institutionalizing the Greenspan policy approach, the Fed would increase the likelihood that future U.S. monetary policy will look like the 1980s and 1990s rather than the 1930s or the 1970s." In summary, "the Fed needs an approach that consolidates the gains of the Greenspan years and ensures that those successful policies will continue—even if future Fed chairmen are less skillful or less committed to price stability than Mr. Greenspan has been."[13]

From the beginning Bernanke has embraced more of a committee approach to decision making. He named Donald Kohn to head up a subcommittee exploring changes in the Fed's communication strategy, even though Kohn was the leading Fed skeptic of Bernanke's inflation-targeting proposal.

Bernanke has also tried to introduce more flexibility into the discussion at meetings. With the oversized nineteen-member committee and lots of presentation materials from the staff, FOMC meetings need to be fairly structured if the work is to be completed, so members usually speak only during their assigned slots. Nonetheless, according to *Wall Street Journal* reporter Greg Ip, Bernanke has tried to encourage more give and take through a signaling system that allows members to interject comments "out of turn."[14] He has made the meetings longer to accommodate a more complete exchange of ideas and he has made the drafting of the Fed's policy directive much more of a collaborative effort.

In a speech in November 2007, Bernanke presented a forceful case for a democratic FOMC:

> An important strength of the Federal Open Market Committee is its diversity. The Board members and Reserve Bank presidents who sit around the table at each meeting of the FOMC bring a wide range of perspectives to the deliberations that reflect the participants' professional backgrounds, the regions of the country with which they are most familiar, and their differing approaches to economic and policy analysis. The task participants face at each meeting is to forge a rough consensus regarding the outlook, the risks to the Committee's objectives, and the appropriate policy response. Of course, it is not always possible—indeed, it would be rather unusual—to come to a set of conclusions that fully represent the views of every participant. But the process of searching for common ground is itself an important aspect of how the Committee operates. Diversity of views drives the Committee to adopt

an eclectic approach and thus serves to limit the risk that a single viewpoint or analytical framework might become unduly dominant."[15]

I agree with Bernanke up to a point: a committee is probably less prone to making big mistakes than is a single decision maker. However, a big committee like the FOMC can have its own problems. Big committees are prone to move slowly in making decisions. Sometimes they are prone to "herd behavior" or "groupthink"—for example, if two speakers in a row express the same view at a meeting, others may decide to fall in line even if they disagree but do not have strong convictions. The result is a "cascading" of agreement—a strong feeling of a consensus at the meeting—even though the conviction level for each individual is very low. A committee can also have trouble communicating clearly if everyone must sign on to the official statements.

BIRD-WATCHING COMES BACK
INTO FASHION

Like other Fed watchers, in the early part of Greenspan's tenure I made a considerable effort to rank FOMC members across the hawk-dove spectrum and then to analyze their public statements relative to this metric. For example, if hawks were sounding especially tough and doves less soft, then the odds of a rate hike could be deemed to be rising. However, as Greenspan's domination became more apparent, I adopted a different tack, and began to divide members into *loyalists*—members who tried to faithfully reproduce Greenspan's views—and *independents*—members who seemed out of sync with Greenspan. I would tend to ignore statements by independents, and focus on loyalist views. Moreover, when the economy was shifting rapidly, I put less weight on the loyalist views if they seemed stale and seemed to reflect Greenspan's older thoughts.

With the change in leadership, the hawk-dove distinction becomes useful again. As expected, the debate at the Fed remains collegial, but more of the disagreements are spilling out in public, through speeches and with more dissents at FOMC meetings. After all, the economic picture is quite complicated, and it would be surprising if FOMC members were in complete agreement. Bernanke stepped in at the second meeting in 2006, and there were four dissents that year and two in 2007.

Figure 10-1 divides the members into hawks and doves—but look for some revisions to this arrangement as glasnost continues to transform the Fed. In practice, I would not put equal weight on the views of all nineteen FOMC members. While everyone speaks at the meetings, only the governors and the president of the New York Fed vote at every meeting. The other four votes rotate among the other eleven presidents on an annual basis. Moreover, some FOMC members focus on other policy issues and have a natural inclination to vote with the chairman. I believe that the key macroeconomists on the board—Ben Bernanke, Frederic Mishkin, and Donald Kohn—carry more weight at the meeting, having the ability to influence members who are not specialists in macroeconomics. Hence, in gauging Fed actions, I put more weight on the "big three."

The Bernanke Fed's new signaling system has already been stress tested and it has not worked very well. In the run-up to the

FIGURE 10-1

Hawk-dove breakdown

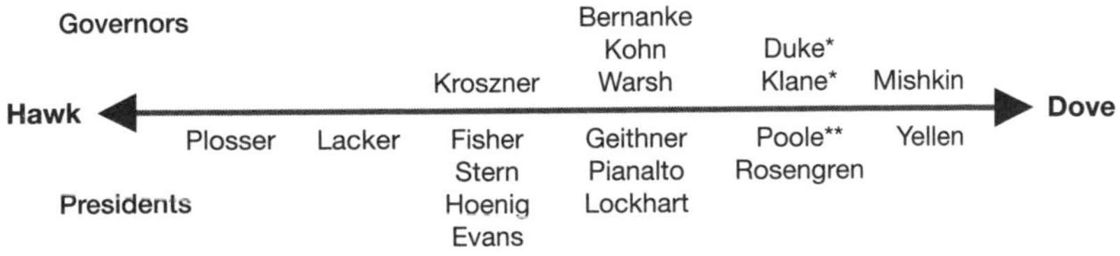

* Pending confirmation
** Retired March 31, 2008

September 2007 FOMC meeting, several regional presidents had suggested the Fed was torn between cutting rates and staying on hold:

> *Dallas President Fisher:* "We have heard much about financial market turbulence . . . Amidst this clamor and drama, some might have lost sight of our economy's great resiliency"[16]

> *Philadelphia President Plosser:* "Disruptions in financial markets can be addressed . . . without necessarily having to make a shift in the overall direction of monetary policy"[17]

> *Richmond President Lacker:* "I still expect consumer spending to be reasonably healthy, and for business investment to continue to expand . . . there are still reasons to remain concerned about the risks to the inflation outlook"[18]

By contrast, Governor Mishkin's speeches focused on the downside risks to the economy. In "Housing and the Monetary Transmission Mechanism," a speech at the Fed's Jackson Hole conference on September 1, 2007, Mishkin explored the downside risks from the housing recession. Two weeks later he talked to the Money Marketeers club in New York about the "Outlook and Risks for the U.S. Economy." After the speech everyone at my table agreed: "That was a 50-basis-point speech." In the event, the Fed cut by 50 basis points. Again, in the run-up to the December FOMC meeting, a number of FOMC members argued strenuously that the Fed wanted to watch and wait rather than cut rates at its upcoming meeting. Then in late November, first Kohn and then Bernanke "marked to market" the Fed's view: "The outlook has . . . been importantly affected over the past month by renewed turbulence in financial markets."[19] In other words, another rate cut is on the table. Sure enough, the Fed cut by 25 basis points on December 11, 2007.

Bernanke is a great believer in policy transparency but, paradoxically, the switch from Greenspan's benevolent dictatorship to Bernanke's democracy makes it harder for the Fed to signal policy changes. In a complex economic environment, it is impossible for a democratic committee to telegraph policy changes in advance, because they themselves will not know the outcome until they have met and discussed the options. Hence in its first two years, the Bernanke Fed has done a poor job of signaling rate moves to the market. As the markets learn to read Bernanke better, the communication problems should diminish some, but it is unlikely that a Bernanke-run Fed will ever telegraph individual funds rate changes as clearly as Greenspan did when he dominated his committee. Democracy can be unpredictable.

11

Zen and the Art of Monetary Maintenance

The Fed's New
Communication Style

Not only has Ben Bernanke changed the internal workings of the Fed, he is also changing the way the Fed presents itself to the public. Greenspan came of age during a period of intense political pressure on the Fed, and he only reluctantly opened the Fed to outside scrutiny. By contrast, Bernanke belongs to a new generation of economists who believe in a fully transparent central bank—that is, the bank should clearly convey to the public its forecasts for the economy, its policy goals, and the rationale behind its policy choices. Yet in another respect, Bernanke is likely to be much less open than Greenspan. Over time Greenspan became an economic guru: his views were widely respected, and he was often drawn into debates outside the purview of the Fed. By contrast, Bernanke will likely present a much lower profile, avoiding issues that could create an appearance of partisanship on the part of the Fed.

PLAIN SPEAKING

Greenspan started to open up the Fed in the second half of his term, but Bernanke is likely to continue much further down the path of clearer communication. In a speech in 2004 he said:

> The research I have discussed today suggests that the central bank should do what it can to make information symmetric, providing the public to the extent possible with the same information that the FOMC uses in making its decisions . . . Besides its policy objectives, the central bank can make other useful information available to the public, including its economic forecasts, its assessment of the economic risks, and (if possible) the models or analytical frameworks that underlie its diagnosis of the economy.
>
> We should continue to seek improvement in each of these areas. For example, FOMC forecasts might be released more frequently and for a longer horizon. Additional variables could be forecasted, notably core inflation, a key factor in FOMC policy decisions. More controversially, the FOMC might consider forecasting future values of the short-term interest rate, as is currently done by the Reserve Bank of New Zealand. The difficulty would be to make clear that an interest-rate forecast is not the same as a policy commitment. The use of "fan charts" to indicate the range of uncertainty would be helpful in this regard; and indeed, providing more information about the range of uncertainty for all FOMC forecasts would be a useful innovation.[1]

Why is this important? Because, says Benanke, "Most importantly, monetary policy makers are public servants whose decisions affect the life of every citizen; consequently, in a democratic society, they have a responsibility to give the people and their elected representatives a full and compelling rationale for the decisions they make. Good communications are a prerequisite if central banks are to maintain the democratic legitimacy and independence that are essential to sound monetary policy making."[2]

Bernanke further states, "Transparency increases the effectiveness of monetary policy and enhances economic and financial performance in several ways:"[3]

- By "improving the public's understanding of the central bank's objectives and policy strategies [it] reduces economic and financial uncertainty and thereby allows businesses and households to make more-informed decisions."

- If investors understand the Fed's objectives, markets will anticipate and reinforce Fed moves. For example, if the markets understand that inflation is exceeding the Fed's target, market interest rates will be bid higher even before the Fed raises the funds rate to cool the economy.

- "Clarity about the central bank's policy objectives and strategy may help anchor the public's long-term inflation expectations, which can substantially improve the efficacy of policy and the overall functioning of the economy."

- "Open discussion of the central bank's analyses and forecasts invites valuable input and feedback from the public."

Bernanke has been gradually introducing greater transparency into the Fed and the markets are already adjusting to a very different information flow. Greenspan tended to speak in Delphic tones and favored ambiguous phrases—"irrational exuberance," "measured pace," "considerable period," "price stability," "firebreak." By contrast, Bernanke's presentation style is clear, if less colorful. In an effort to be transparent, he has not hesitated to suggest numerical ranges for key economic parameters:

- At the start of the tightening cycle, Greenspan said, "when we arrive at neutral we will know it." Bernanke suggested that the neutral funds rate could be in the 3.7 to 4.7 percent range.

- Greenspan argued that "price stability is best thought of as an environment in which inflation is so low and stable over time that it does not materially enter into the decisions of households and firms." Bernanke argued for a range of 1 to 2 percent on the core PCE.

Bernanke has also hinted at estimates for other key parameters: the inflation neutral unemployment rate or NAIRU is about 5 percent and the long-run trend growth in the economy is about 3 percent. Bernanke does not hold religiously to any of these numbers, but uses them to clarify the logic of his arguments.

While Bernanke is a much clearer speaker than Greenspan, the markets have had trouble adapting to the new style because they are used to looking for secret messages. When Bernanke talked about alternative monetary policy tools to deal with deflation (a general fall in prices) in 2003, many in the markets put on their Greenspan decoder rings and concluded, "If he is talking about deflation as a *possibility* it must mean it is *likely.*" A similar episode occurred in the spring of 2006 when he hinted that the Fed might pause at some point in its rate hike cycle. The response in the market was: "If he is saying they *may* pause it must mean that they *are* pausing!" After all, that is exactly the way Greenspan would have dropped such a hint. However, Bernanke quickly revealed that "possibly" means "possibly," "may" means "may," and "at some point" means "at some point." My advice to investors: it is time to sell your Greenspan decoder ring on eBay.

THE GURU IS GONE

While Bernanke wants to open up the Fed's policy and forecasting process to public view, he wants to lower the Fed chairman's profile on issues unrelated to monetary policy. In the second half of his chairmanship, Alan Greenspan became not only the world's most powerful central banker, but the world's best-known expert on a variety of topics unrelated to monetary policy. Congress and the public increasingly looked to him for advice on everything from curing poverty to education reform. In their otherwise complimentary paper on Greenspan, Blinder and Reis argue that his comments on specific fiscal policy options compromised the independence of the Fed: "If Congress is supposed to stay out of monetary policy, then the Fed should stay out of fiscal policy and other political matters."[4] Greenspan's guru status unnecessarily exposed the Fed to political backlash.

Bernanke does not want to be seen as an economic guru. At his confirmation hearing in November 2005, he sidestepped questions on fiscal policy, saying, "That's outside the realm of my authority." True to form, in his first two years on the job Bernanke has offered his general support for low budget deficits, free trade, and other basic tenets of mainstream economics, but he has avoided commenting on specific policies.

A ONE-EIGHTY

The new communication model is literally a 180-degree shift from the old model of central banking. The new model asks central bankers to be clear and accountable for sometimes unpopular decisions. Is this being naively idealistic? Doesn't it risk the Fed's treasured independence? I don't think so—I think this is the right direction in which to move. Ultimately, the Fed will maintain its independence by acting like a nonpartisan institution. The old communication model made it look like the Fed had something to hide, that it had some secret political agenda, or that it was covering up its mistakes. The greatest danger to the Fed came in the late 1970s and early 1980s when it let inflation get out of hand, forcing it to implement deeply unpopular policies and inviting claims of professional incompetence. However, if the Fed "sticks to its knitting"—pre-empting inflation before it runs out of control, smoothing the business cycle, and avoiding being drawn into political areas such tax policy—I believe it is a strong enough institution to be judged on its record.

12

See No Evil, Hear No Evil, Speak No Evil

The Policy Response to an Asset Market Bubble

One of the most controversial questions in central banking is how policy makers should factor asset markets into their decision making.[1] As I noted in chapter 3, there is widespread agreement that asset prices are an important part of the monetary policy transmission mechanism—that is, changes in Fed policy are transmitted to or impact the economy by stimulating or depressing asset markets. During a sustained boom in the housing or stock market, households feel wealthier and are likely to spend more. They also have more collateral to offer when applying for loans, making it easier to borrow. Similarly, when the stock market or commercial real estate is booming, businesses also have more collateral, which also encourages spending. The opposite occurs when asset prices are falling. There is little disagreement that central banks must take these effects into account when deciding monetary policy.

The tough policy challenge comes in the extreme environment of a suspected asset price bubble or bust. Should a central bank step in to try to stop an unsustainable surge in asset prices? And, should the bubble burst, how long should a central bank wait before cutting interest rates? The controversy arises for two reasons. First, if the Fed focuses on managing asset markets, it may compromise its other goals. The Fed has only one major policy tool (changing the funds rate) and a few much less effective secondary tools (verbal persuasion, changing regulations, and lending out liquid assets). It can't be fully effective in managing the economy if it focuses on managing asset markets.

Second, when policy makers attempt to manage the markets they distort the behavior of investors and create a number of inefficiencies. The most important distortion is moral hazard (see chapter 6). In the 1990s this moral hazard problem introduced a new term into the financial lexicon: "the Greenspan put."[2] At the height of the stock market boom, some investors came to believe (incorrectly) that stock investing was a sure thing, because the Fed would prevent any serious downward movement in the market. In fact, the stock market collapsed in 2000–2001, despite Fed easing—and yet, some investors still cling to the idea of a Greenspan—and now, Bernanke—put.

Policy makers have three choices in dealing with suspected asset bubbles. The classical approach is to set policy on the path appropriate for the economy and ignore both the bubble and its bursting. By this view, any direct action by the central bank is interfering with the free market. Booms and busts teach investors about appropriate risk management. Moreover, stopping a bust prevents the purging process of removing rot from the financial system.

The second approach is *asymmetric risk management*. If bubbles are very hard to identify and manage, then rather than try to control them, the Fed should allow a possible bubble to run its course, and tighten monetary policy only to the extent that the booming asset market is stimulating economic activity. If the asset boom turns out to be a bubble, and it pops, proponents of asymmetric risk management believe the Fed should then ease aggressively to avoid a serious blow to the economy. The medical analogy would be: spend very little on preventative care, but have a state-of-the-art emergency room to deal with big problems when they arise.

The third approach—which I favor—is to both lean against suspected bubbles and take aggressive action if and when the bubble bursts. In this view, the Fed should be able to identify a high risk of a bubble and lean against a suspected bubble by raising the funds rate a bit more than it would otherwise. If and when the bubble bursts, the Fed should respond with aggressive easing. In other words, the third approach is to use an ounce of prevention *and* a pound of cure.

BERNANKE'S ASYMMETRIC APPROACH

The top ranks of the Fed generally agree with the asymmetric approach to asset market bubbles. Greenspan argues for it: "The notion that a well-timed incremental tightening could have been calibrated to prevent the late 1990s bubble is almost surely illusion."[3] Former governor Laurence Meyer sees many problems with "preemptive strikes against bubbles."[4] Bernanke believes the only preventative medicine should be ensuring that financial institutions are properly "prepared for the contingency of a large shock to asset prices."[5] Vice Chairman Donald Kohn agrees: policy should be "motivated not by the desire to achieve any particular level of asset prices, but rather by the Federal Reserve's assessment of how changes in asset prices were affecting the forecast for growth and inflation."[6]

Bernanke et al. see three problems with preemptive strikes against bubbles: they are hard to identify, policy responses can be poorly timed, and the Fed does not have the right tools to deal with bubbles.

> *The identification problem:* Bernanke argues that it is frequently difficult to identify an asset price bubble in real time. The fundamental value of a stock, for example, is determined by two unobservable factors—"the dividends that investors

expect to receive and the risk premiums they require to hold stocks." Moreover, he notes, "To declare that a bubble exists, the Fed must not only be able to accurately estimate the unobservable fundamentals underlying equity valuations, it must have confidence that it can do so better than the financial professionals whose collective information is reflected in asset markets."[7] Rapid asset price appreciation does not prove that there is a bubble—after all, many things increase in price over time, while relatively few things actually collapse. Even economists frequently disagree when it comes to bubbles: where some see strong fundamentals, others see bubbles.

Lots of lags: Even if a bubble is identified, policy responses can be poorly timed. It takes time to identify a potential bubble; it takes additional time to agree on a policy change; and it takes yet more time for those actions to affect the markets and the economy. In other words, there is a *recognition lag* and a *policy impact lag*. This means that there is a high risk that policy efforts to stop the bubble will kick in just as the bubble is deflating of its own accord. Policy could end up doing more harm than good.

Difficulty in popping: Bernanke believes that it is very difficult to safely pop a bubble. Indeed, deflating a bubble is like "doing brain surgery with a sledgehammer."[8] He argues, "My suggested framework for Fed policy regarding asset-market instability can be summarized by the adage, Use the right tool for the job . . . as a general rule, the Fed will do best by focusing its monetary policy instruments on achieving its macro goals—price stability and maximum sustainable employment—while using its regulatory, supervisory, and lender-of-last resort powers to help ensure financial stability."[9] This is because most bubbles contain very strong expectation components—prices go up because everyone expects them to go up—that make them easy to inflate but difficult to safely deflate. Moreover, bubbles often deflate precipitously on their own—without help from tighter monetary policy.

Plausible deniability: I would add a fourth argument for stepping aside in the face of a potential bubble: attempting to deflate the bubble would expose the Fed to political backlash. The Fed does not want blood on its hands when the markets retrench; it would rather that the markets suffered self-inflicted wounds. Of course, the tougher it is to identify and influence a bubble, the greater the risk of a policy mistake and the greater the risk of a political fallout. In the central banking community there is a passionate belief in the importance of maintaining independence from political pressure: ultimately policy choices have to be weighed against the risk of the Fed losing its independence.

In his academic days, Bernanke coauthored a paper with Mark Gertler that formally tested the costs and benefits of trying to control asset bubbles.[10] Gertler presented this paper at the Fed's annual conference in Jackson Hole, Wyoming, in 1999. In the standard model of Fed behavior, called the *Taylor rule,* the Fed is assumed to respond only to two things: changes in price inflation and changes in the degree of slack in the economy. Adjusting the standard Taylor rule to include stock prices, Bernanke and Gertler found that the economy performed best when the Fed put little or no weight on stock prices in its policy decisions. In other words, reacting to movements in stock prices does little to smooth out output and inflation variability. Instead, they find that the best model for policy—the model that produces the least volatility in either inflation or output—is one that focuses on price stability first, slack in the economy second, and the stock market a distant third.

THE LEADER DOTH PROTEST TOO MUCH

What do I make of the Fed's approach to asset market bubbles? There is no question that asset bubbles pose a difficult challenge to central banks. Nonetheless, I still see a case for a lean-against-the-bubble strategy. Monetary policy is all about making judgments using imperfect models and information. All of the problems that arise in countering asset market bubbles—imprecise models, policy lags, political ramifications of putting a check on market exuberance, and the need for a risk-management approach—also apply when the Fed is raising interest rates to cool off an overheating economy. If a bubble seems likely, a risk-managing Fed should lean against it.

Asset bubbles are, admittedly, hard to identify, and there are many instances of premature warnings. A good recent example is Alan Greenspan's suggestion in the mid-1990s that there could be "irrational exuberance" in the stock market. That warning came in a speech in December 1996, three years before the peak in the Dow Jones Industrial Average (figure 12-1). Yet even after the stock market collapse in 2000–2001, the market never dropped below the December 1996 level. In all likelihood, Greenspan's hunch that there was a bubble in the market was premature, although it seems equally likely that the market did go into a bubble a couple years later.

While it is hard to identify a bubble with certainty, it is possible to identify a high risk of a bubble. Consider the recent housing

FIGURE 12-1

The Dow Jones Industrial Average

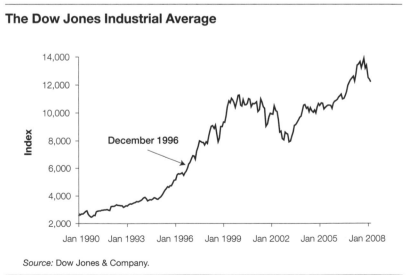

Source: Dow Jones & Company.

boom, bubble, and bust. When I became chief U.S. economist at Lehman Brothers in 2002, there was already talk of a possible bubble in the housing market. Initially, my colleagues and I were skeptical and argued that talk of a housing bubble at the national level was exaggerated.[11] We agreed with Bernanke that making a case for a bubble requires more than simple pricing metrics.

Robert Shiller, an economist made famous for predicting the 2000 stock market crash, argued that the U.S. housing bubble started as early as 1998, when home price inflation began to exceed consumer price inflation. However, our view was that a better gauge of home price sustainability was a comparison with income growth (figure 12-2). By this metric, the initial pick-up in prices was a catching up for weak growth early in the 1990s. Moreover, lower interest rates and new mortgage products were making homes more affordable. In our judgment, the initial rise in home prices was driven by fundamental factors—such as lower mortgage rates and a strong economy—rather than irrational exuberance. We were with the majority who believed Shiller's warnings were premature.

FIGURE 12-2

Home price growth and income growth—a comparison

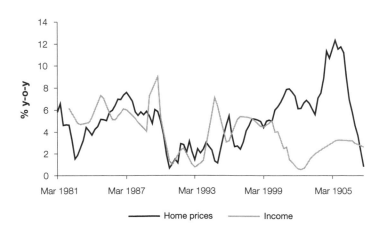

Source: Office of Federal Housing Enterprise Oversight; Department of Commerce.

Starting in 2004, however, we changed our tune. The case for a bubble was not just strong home price inflation, but three warning signals of aggressive speculative behavior:

- There was a surge in the use of hybrid mortgages, which required no money down, demanded little documentation of income or assets, or offered low initial "teaser" rates of payment.

- There was a surge in the number of buyers who were self-identified speculators, or "flippers." These flippers were particularly active in the hot markets. After all, to make money flipping, property prices have to be rising fast enough to cover the relatively high real estate transaction costs (broker fees, closing costs, inspections, etc.). Thus if transaction costs were 5 percent of the price of a house, and a buyer wanted to flip properties every three months, generating a positive return required more than 20 percent annual price appreciation.

- Hot markets were getting hotter. We found that, on average, metro areas with home price inflation of 5 percent at the start of 2004 accelerated to 7 percent a year later, while cities with 20 percent inflation accelerated to 28 percent inflation. It is no coincidence that a Web site called condoflip.com was set up to trade Florida real estate in 2005 . . . and was defunct two years later.[12]

BEER BREWERS' DELIGHT? "FROTH" IN THE MARKETS

By July 2005, even Alan Greenspan was willing to admit to localized bubbles: "Whether home prices on average for the nation as a whole are overvalued . . . is difficult to ascertain, but there do appear to be, at a minimum, signs of froth in some local markets."[13] While the word *froth* sounds more like the description of a head on a beer

than a serious problem, in his usual coded fashion Greenspan implicitly admitted that the Fed could identify a likely bubble. Moreover, in the recent publicity tour for his memoirs, Greenspan now says that froth "was a euphemism for a bubble [and] all the froth bubbles add up to an aggregate bubble."[14] So much for the identification problem.

So how should a central bank safely and effectively resist a bubble? Again, I disagree with Fed officials. Greenspan now claims he attempted to suppress the housing bubble. However, I do not believe his heart was in the effort. Greenspan insisted that the Fed slowly hike interest rates by 25 basis points for fourteen meetings in a row. The cumulative rate hikes—4.25 percentage points by the time Bernanke stopped hiking in the summer of 2006—look impressive on the surface. On closer inspection, however, the rate hikes are less impressive. First, rate hikes cool growth only if they cool off asset markets: and asset markets (including housing) continued to boom despite the Fed's hikes. Second, as John Taylor pointed out at the 2007 Jackson Hole conference, the Fed hiked rates much more slowly than a typical Taylor rule would warrant.[15]

Figure 12-3 compares the actual path of the funds rate to a Taylor rule, where the Fed is assumed to respond to unemployment and core PCE inflation. The model suggests the Fed was right to cut rates through the middle of 2003 but, as the economy recovered, it should have hiked much faster. Thus, for the last two and a half years of Greenspan's chairmanship, the funds rate was too low relative to trends in the economy, and only with the last three hikes by Bernanke did the Fed get back to where it should have been. Of course, policy making is more complicated than merely looking at the unemployment rate and core inflation, but it is not clear why Greenspan did not lean harder against a very growth-friendly financial environment.

Moreover, the tightening was not only slow, but was sugar-coated with promises that the moves would be measured and designed not to restrain the economy, but to bring interest rates back to normal. Speeches from Fed officials downplayed the likelihood of a bubble, pointing to local "froth" and "unconnected markets." In

FIGURE 12-3

The funds rate: Actual and Taylor rule predictions

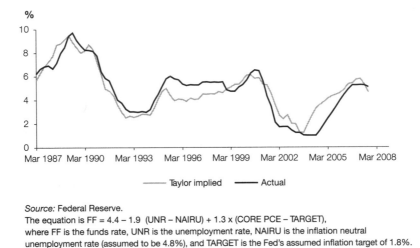

Source: Federal Reserve.
The equation is FF = 4.4 – 1.9 (UNR – NAIRU) + 1.3 x (CORE PCE – TARGET),
where FF is the funds rate, UNR is the unemployment rate, NAIRU is the inflation neutral
unemployment rate (assumed to be 4.8%), and TARGET is the Fed's assumed inflation target of 1.8%.

a speech in June 2005, Greenspan argued that housing markets are inherently local, and therefore unlikely to turn down in a synchronous fashion. More important, home price inflation accelerated as the Fed hiked. As I noted earlier, monetary policy does not work by magic, but by constraining or hurting asset markets. Had the Fed been more attuned to the housing bubble, there would have been fewer speeches about how hard bubbles are to identify and perhaps a 50-basis-point hike thrown into the mix to grab market attention.

Greenspan has written an op-ed piece for the _Financial Times_ with the emphatic title "The Fed is blameless on the property bubble."[16] He argues that the Fed can not be blamed because housing bubbles "emerged in more than two dozen countries between 2001 and 2006" and therefore the cause had to be global in nature. He points to the worldwide drop in interest rates and aggressive investor behavior as the culprits. While I have some sympathy with this view—I don't think the Fed was the main reason for the bubble—I believe the Fed did play a role. Bubbles are more likely in smaller housing markets, but it is virtually unheard of for the huge diversified U.S. housing market to have a bubble. It is more appropriate to compare the major U.S. regional bubbles—such as in California—to the bubbles in overseas economies like Australia and Denmark. By this metric, the United States had a number of bubbles that were bigger than average. Moreover, the Fed plays a leading role in setting not just U.S. interest rates, but global interest rates. It is probably the case that the Fed's failure to react to signs of a housing bubble in the United States contributed to the global housing bubble as well.

Fear of political backlash is an argument for moving cautiously in the face of a likely bubble, but is not a reason to ignore the bubble. Being a party pooper, so to speak, is part of the Fed's mandate. Fed actions to fight inflation are a significant factor in most recessions. If the Fed can, in the colorful words of Chairman William McChesney Martin, "take away the punch bowl" when the economic party gets too wild, why can't they water down the punch when a party in the markets is getting out of hand? Isn't the Fed more susceptible to political attack if it allows a destabilizing event like an asset bubble to form and then pop?

The reason it makes sense to lean against a likely bubble is that cleaning up the mess—like bubble gum in your hair—can be very difficult. As the bubble deflates, the Fed initially stands aside—it doesn't want to reward excessive risk takers and prevent a return to normal market valuations. However, often the markets overshoot, selling off far below fair value as panic settles in. Beyond the risks to short-run growth, the bubble leaves a legacy of overspending and overborrowing for the assets in question (e.g., too much investment in tech hardware in the late 1990s and too much home building more recently). Fed easing can mitigate, but it cannot stop, serious damage to the economy.

WHEN IT POPS

So much for the inflation side of the bubble; what about the deflation side? As I noted above, the classical purge-the-rot view is that the Fed should not respond to bubbles at all, but allow the markets to learn their lessons on their own. This was the liquidationist hypothesis of Andrew Mellon, Treasury secretary before the Great Depression: "Liquidate labor, liquidate stocks, liquidate the farmers, liquidate real estate." Even panic was not altogether a bad thing. His Scrooge-like view: "It will purge the rottenness out of the system. High costs of living and high living will come down. People will work harder, live a more moral life. Values will be adjusted, and enterprising people will pick up the wrecks from less competent people."[17]

Fortunately, few economists today believe in ignoring the markets when they collapse. Instead, central banks perform a tightrope act. On the one hand, they do not want to stop corrections in the markets that penalize excessive risk taking; on the other hand, they do not want to allow a level of financial market pain that will push the economy into a recession. The issue is not whether the Fed steps in during a financial crisis, but how much pain it allows before it steps in.

I'm not a big fan of the Bernanke and Greenspan's "see no evil" approach to potential asset bubbles (making no attempt to lean against a suspected bubble) nor do I like the "speak no evil" approach (giving speeches that either deny that a bubble exists or deny that a bubble is identifiable) or the "hear no evil" approach (Greenspan rebuffed suggestions that the Fed investigate inappropriate lending practices). I also believe it is better for the Fed to remain silent about its assessment of asset prices rather than actively argue against a bubble. I think the Fed should adopt a policy of leaning against suspected bubbles. Even if the modest tightening fails to stop the boom, by making the funds rate higher than it would otherwise be and by lowering inflation a bit, it creates more room for the Fed to cut rates should boom turn into bust, dragging down the economy. While I'm critical of their response to bubbles, I think the Fed generally does the right thing when asset markets collapse. I think it makes sense to at first allow the market to unwind, but then to step in aggressively if the market "correction" becomes disorderly and threatens to seriously damage the economy.

13

Radical Risk Management

A New Policy Focus for the Fed

Most of Ben Bernanke's agenda for change at the Fed—inflation targeting, plain speaking, a more democratic committee, more reliance on models and research, and a lower profile for the chairman—was clear as he entered the job. Perhaps the biggest surprise has been his strong embrace of a risk-management approach to policy—that is, basing policy not just on the most likely outcome for the economy, but also on the risks around that outcome. Other central bankers, including Alan Greenspan, also believed in risk management, but the Bernanke Fed has taken risk management to a new level.

I believe an aggressive approach to risk management is a natural result of two parts of Bernanke's background. First, his research on the financial accelerator model has made him particularly sensitive to the disruptions to banks and the credit markets. The recent combination of tightening credit, falling asset values, and a weakening economy could produce exactly the nasty negative feedback loop that financial accelerator models predict. Second, his study of the Great Depression makes him particularly aware of the dangers when the Fed does not act to stop a banking collapse.

SON OF SMOOTH

In a normal economic environment both Bernanke and Greenspan favor a *gradualist* approach to monetary policy. Uncertainty about the economic outlook and how the economy will respond to policy encourages policy makers to move gradually—changing the funds rate in small increments. Often with the benefit of 20-20 hindsight the Fed is accused of moving too slowly in response to changes in the economy—"we knew the housing market was going to collapse, why did the Fed wait for it to happen before cutting?" In reality things are rarely this black and white, so the Fed tends to move slowly, usually raising or lowering interest rates in 25-basis-point moves. Under Greenspan, two-thirds of the changes in the funds target were by 25 basis points. Moreover, this focus on 25 basis points increased over time: in their joint final tightening cycle, the Greenspan- and Bernanke-led Feds between them raised the funds rate 25 basis points for seventeen meetings in a row. The largest move the Fed made in the Greenspan era was the 75-basis-point rate hike in November 1994.

As a Fed governor, Bernanke argued that gradualism is not only empirically a good description of policy, but also that such smoothing of interest rates is a desirable feature of monetary policy. Specifically, he sees three reasons for gradualism: "(1) Policymakers' uncertainty about the economy should lead to more gradual adjustment of the policy rate; (2) gradualism in adjusting the policy rate affords policymakers greater influence over the long-term interest rates that most affect the economy; and (3) gradualism reduces risks to financial stability."[1] I would add that smooth rate moves gives the Fed a strong reputation for having a steady hand on the tiller.

Gradual policy changes help move longer-term interest rates because if investors know the Fed moves gradually, they will anticipate cycles of interest rate hikes and cuts. For example, if the Fed is at the start of an interest rate hiking cycle, investors will anticipate that the funds rate and other short-term borrowing rates will be higher in the future. They will buy longer-term securities only if those securities pay a yield that matches the average of future short-term rates. For example, if the funds rate is 2 percent today and investors expect it to rise to 4 percent next year, they will buy a two-year interest-earning asset only if it matches the 3 percent expected average for the funds rate.

DESPERATE TIMES CALL FOR
DESPERATE MEASURES

As a Fed governor, Ben Bernanke has also talked about the exceptions to the gradualist approach.[2] He argues from a risk-management point of view that if there is a high cost for failing to move quickly, the Fed should abandon the go-slow approach and move aggressively. He cites the rapid 2001 easing cycle as an example. During that period the Fed faced a collapsing stock market, and quickly cut interest rates in an attempt to forestall recession; it would have been risky to move more slowly.

A key motivation for the risk-management approach is concern about uncertainty in the economy. In a speech he gave in 2007 Bernanke highlighted three areas of uncertainty:[3]

1. Uncertainty about "the current state of the economy." He noted, "At best, official data represent incomplete snapshots of various aspects of the economy, and even then they may be released with a substantial lag and be revised later."

2. Uncertainty about "the structure of the economy (including the transmission mechanism of monetary policy)." For example, there is considerable uncertainty about how effective policy changes will be in moving asset markets and about key threshold variables such as the level of unemployment that triggers inflation pressure.

3. And uncertainty about "the way in which private agents form expectations about future economic developments

and policy actions." For example, recall the discussion of
the modern Phillips Curve in chapter 2: if workers and
firms have no faith in the Fed's anti-inflation resolve, they
will quickly extrapolate any inflation pressures into their
own wage and price decisions, creating an upward spiral
of inflation.

This speech drew on a relatively new economics literature arguing for a risk-management approach to policy. Working his way
through this complicated literature, Bernanke noted how a number
of studies suggest that "the concern about worst-case scenarios em-
phasized by the robust-control approach may likewise lead to am-
plification rather than attenuation in the response of the optimal
policy to shocks." Or more simply, "Intuition suggests that stronger
action by the central bank may be warranted to prevent particularly
costly outcomes."[4]

On a practical level, what do these views mean for policy in
2008? The risk scenario concentrating the Fed's mind in late 2007
and 2008 was an adverse feedback loop. Bernanke himself has not
said a lot about this, with good reason: for the Fed chairman to
clearly lay out a worst-case scenario for the economy would surely
scare the markets and become a self-fulfilling proposition. That
would not be good risk management.

Bernanke left it to one of his lieutenants, Frederic Mishkin, to
gently present the downside scenario. In a series of speeches, starting with the Jackson Hole conference in August 2007, Mishkin laid
out the downside risks to the economy. His worry: an adverse feedback loop would develop between tightening credit conditions,
asset prices, and the economy, as in the housing market. The sharp
pullback in lending to subprime borrowers has caused a sharp drop
in demand for homes. This weaker demand means falling home
prices. Falling home prices means more homes have negative equity (i.e., the value of the home is less than the value of the mortgage) creating an incentive for people to default on their loan. Loan
defaults mean more houses are being resold into the market at bar-
gain prices, pushing home prices lower. Meanwhile, the weakness

in the housing market means falling home construction and weaker consumer spending. Completing the loop, the weaker economy weakens home demand further. Even with a benign baseline forecast for growth, a risk-managing central bank may decide aggressive rate cuts needed to short-circuit this adverse feedback loop. If the adverse feedback does not happen, the Fed can then quickly rescind the rate cuts.

RISKY BUSINESS

Of course a risk-management policy is not without its own risks—it undercuts the Fed's attempts to be more predictable. The baseline forecasts the Fed presents four times a year under its new communication strategy are of little use in predicting where a risk-managing Fed is headed. Moreover, the central bank must explain exactly what it is doing without presenting confidence-sapping scenarios in speeches.

It is hard to properly calibrate a risk-management policy. If the Fed feels no restraints on how quickly it raises or lowers rates, a risk-management approach could lead to a quite unstable policy. Monetary policy works with long and variable lags, so if the economy is weakening, the weakness can only be quickly reversed if the bank cuts aggressively (providing immediate help to the economy) and then takes back the eases later (to avoid overstimulating the economy over the longer term as policy effects build). Attempting to perfectly smooth out the growth in the economy would require dramatic swings in policy.

Risk management may undercut the confidence-building component of monetary policy. If the markets view policy as erratic or unpredictable, they may become more worried rather than reassured by Fed rate cuts. If the bond market begins to doubt the Fed's anti-inflation resolve, rate cuts could cause higher rather than lower bond yields, undercutting some of the policy stimulus.

There are also exit strategy problems for a risk-managing central bank. By its nature a risk-managing policy is front-loaded: the

Fed eases more upfront to forestall an adverse feedback loop. But once the Fed starts moving quickly, the markets will get used to the idea that the Fed is delivering big rate cuts. Ultimately the market could overshoot and expect too much from the Fed, selling off if the Fed fails to deliver. The Fed must also prepare to rescind the super-easy policy quickly if the risky scenario does not materialize. Otherwise the economy will overheat. In 2007 and 2008 a number of Fed officials acknowledged these risks and warned the markets of potentially rapid hikes in the future. A too-slow removal of an emergency easing can create problems—that was exactly Greenspan's mistake in 2004 and 2005.

Monetary policy should account for not just the most likely outcome for the economy, but also the risks that outcome entails. However, a risk-management approach to policy can create confusion in the markets, is hard to calibrate, and is hard to exit from. Risk management puts a premium on good communication, particularly if the markets expect gradualism and if the central bank lacks the full confidence of the markets. The Bernanke Fed will no doubt continue to adopt an aggressive risk management approach. If they are to avoid unwanted volatility in the markets they will have a lot of explaining to do to both the capital markets and the general public.

PART IV

BERNANKE'S BEGINNING

The Early Report Card

Ben Bernanke has faced some intense (and as we will see, often unwarranted) criticism in his short tenure. On Wall Street trading floors and in the business press he has earned some rather nasty nicknames: "Helicopter Ben," "B-52 Ben," "Bearnanke," and "NASCAR" Bernanke (because of the speed of rate cuts in January 2008). In the Wall Street Journal's *periodic polls, economists initially gave him an overall grade of B– or B (between 80 and 85 on a scale of 100), but in February 2008 his grade dipped to a C (a 75).[1] Note, however, that his "classmates" have been doing as bad or worse. Compared with the October 2006 survey, European Central Bank President Jean-Claude Trichet's grade plunged to 75 from 90, Bank of England Governor Mervyn King's rating dipped to 70 from 78, and the U.S. secretary of the Treasury, Henry Paulson, earned a 74, down from 87. In other words, all these gentlemen are getting "C's."*

Realistically, since Bernanke has little more than two years on his belt, it's really not fair to give his Fed any grade other than an incomplete. Taking a two-year slice out of any Fed chair's career will include some great periods for the economy and some awful periods (the exception is G. William Miller, whose one-and-a-half-year term was purely in the latter category). As I will show, there are some valid reasons to criticize the Bernanke Fed—most important, Fed communication has been quite poor. However, Bernanke inherited an extremely challenging policy environment from Alan Greenspan. He has had to perform not one, but two, balancing acts—forestalling both inflation and a recession and providing the right support to capital markets without creating serious moral hazards. The Fed has only one policy "hand"—raising or lowering interest rates—to juggle these four balls.

In chapter 14, I argue that we should judge the Bernanke Fed on the possible, not the impossible: the Fed cannot both ease policy to fight recession and capital market collapse and tighten policy to stop inflation and avoid bailing out risky investments. It cannot yet be determined whether the Fed has made the best of a bad situation. On a similar note, the Fed should be judged based on real-time knowledge—what other economists and financial markets experts are seeing—rather than 20-20 hindsight. I then turn in chapter 15 to two key concerns: the Fed's ongoing communication problems and the political risks facing the Fed. Finally, I share my thoughts on the outlook in the conclusion.

14

Murphy's Law

New Fed Chairmen Always Seem to Face a Tough Environment

When Ben Bernanke succeeded Alan Greenspan at the Fed in February 2006, the conventional view was that he was inheriting a relatively benign economic, financial, and policy outlook. Certainly there were rumblings of a bubble in the housing market—even Alan Greenspan had admitted to regional "froth"—and with strong commodity prices there was some concern about inflation. However, most economists were optimistic. In a Bloomberg survey of economists that month the average forecaster expected GDP growth of 3.1 percent in the year ahead, with consumer price inflation of 2.6 percent and the Fed funds rate steady at 4.75 percent. None of the seventy-six respondents expected a recession in the next year and a half.[1]

INTERESTING TIMES

Unfortunately, there seems to be a form of Murphy's Law at work when it comes to new Fed chairmen: their term always seems to co-incide with a challenging time for the economy and financial markets. Paul Volcker stepped in at the most challenging point in modern Fed history: in the face of massive political pressure and with inflation running out of control he was obliged to stomp on the monetary policy brakes immediately. A good simple gauge of the economic challenges facing the Fed is the misery index—the sum of the unemployment rate and year-over-year consumer price inflation (figure 14-1). When Volcker took action in 1979, the misery index jumped to its post–World War II high of 22 percent. Greenspan also took over at a challenging time: inflation was creeping higher, the Fed was gradually providing resistance, and just a few months into the job, Greenspan had to handle the 1987 stock market crash. The misery index picked up in 1989, but never approached the levels under Volcker.

In a perfect example of Murphy's Law, Bernanke stepped into the job at just the wrong moment. Greenspan had let the economy,

FIGURE 14-1

The misery index

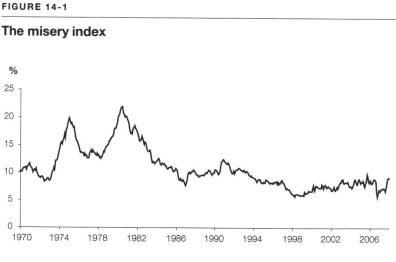

Source: Bureau of Labor Statistics.

the housing market, and the credit market run too hot at the end of his chairmanship. As a result, Bernanke inherited both a modest inflation problem and bubbles in the housing and credit markets. Moreover, the capital markets crisis proved to be much more complicated and persistent than past crises. The two big financial events Greenspan faced, the 1987 stock market crash and the 1998 freeze up in fixed income markets, were relatively easy to fix. In each case a few rate cuts—and in the latter case, a semibailout of one troubled firm—were enough to restore normalcy to the markets. The mix of growth, inflation, and financial markets problems Bernanke inherited falls short of what Volcker walked into, but it is a lot tougher than what Greenspan faced.

This was bad news for Bernanke, but good news for someone trying to learn quickly about him (although there have been a few weekends where I wished I was writing in less interesting times). The challenging economic and market environment at the start of Bernanke's term has provided a rich natural experiment for demonstrating how the new chairman will operate. My fellow Fed watchers and I knew he could talk the talk: Bernanke has a great pedigree for the job and, as we have seen, he had no shortage of ideas on how to improve monetary policy. But would he walk the walk? Or more precisely, given the rapidly evolving economic and financial environment, would he survive running the gauntlet? In this chapter, I'll look at the challenging environment Bernanke's Fed faced and how he reacted.

SON OF STAGFLATION

Bernanke inherited a mild case of stagflation. Within weeks of his stepping into the job, data for the core PCE deflator was revised up; it had been showing inflation within Bernanke's comfort zone, but with the revisions it was running above that bound. At the same time the housing market began to unravel; it started with a weakening in demand in the first half of 2006, followed by a sharp recession in home construction starting in the summer of 2006, and finally a drop in home prices beginning in 2007. Despite the housing woes, the overall economy remained healthy through the third quarter of 2007: indeed, GDP growth outside of residential construction actually accelerated (figure 14-2). But by the beginning of 2008 the economy appeared to be sliding into recession.

This stagflation has both cyclical and secular components. After many years of false alarms, it appears that a sustained commodity scarcity has arrived, putting upward pressure on the real price of commodities. It is also cyclical: normally in the later stages of a business expansion—as demand for commodities and workers become strong—consumer prices inflation begins to pick-up. It takes time for economic weakness to create enough slack in the labor market and the economy in general to reverse the rise in inflation. In the meantime, the economy suffers both higher unemployment and higher inflation. Stagflation poses a no-win situation for a central bank. The inflationary forces argue for tight monetary policy, while the weak economy argues for easier monetary policy. The Fed cannot be simultaneously tight and easy.

Adding to the challenge, Bernanke also inherited a fragile financial environment. In 2006 the markets for mortgage debt con-

FIGURE 14-2

GDP growth: Total and excluding home construction

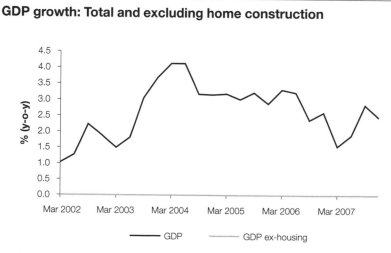

Source: Department of Commerce.

tinued to perform well despite the sharp drop in home demand and deceleration in home price inflation. That Indian summer ended in February 2007 with the collapse of the subprime mortgage market, as investors became increasingly aware of the poor quality of the underlying assets. For the next several months the rest of the credit market was in limbo, but then starting in July and continuing to the day of this writing there has been a steady drumbeat of shocks to the financial system. Each month investors learn about a new troubled part of the capital markets: asset-backed commercial paper, structured investment vehicles, monolines, auction rate securities, and so forth—all have had their day of infamy (this will be discussed later in the chapter). These repeated negative surprises sapped the confidence out of the economy and financial markets.

GREENSPAN'S NEW ROLE: KIBITZER

Bernanke faced one additional challenge that Greenspan did not have: implicit criticism from his more famous predecessor. When Volcker resigned, he became an investment banker, turned his attention to other forms of public service, and refrained from commenting on the economy or monetary policy. By contrast, having returned to the consulting business, Greenspan has become a powerful commentator on the economy; and, while he has been careful to avoid direct comments on monetary policy, investors can read between the lines. Greenspan's very visible comments have even earned a rebuke from the head of the Bank of England, Mervyn King. Commenting on his predecessor, Eddie George, he said: "I am very grateful to Eddie George for not being on the radio or in the newspapers commenting on what the Monetary Policy Committee is doing," King said. "In due course I will do the same."[2]

Greenspan has been warning of both inflation risks and impending recession. In early 2007 he argued for a one-in-three risk of recession before year-end. In the event, the economy refused to slow on cue, but Greenspan remained undeterred, upping the probability to "close to 50 percent."[3] The astute reader will ask: if

Greenspan is saying that there is a 50 percent probability of recession, isn't he suggesting that the Fed is behind the curve and should be cutting interest rates faster to reduce that probability? However, Greenspan's message is a bit more subtle, and a lot more ominous, because he also sees a major risk of inflation. He believes that the recent rise in the price of imports from China is a sign that this important restraint on U.S. inflation is fading. This, in turn, could trigger an ugly sequence of events. Holding inflation to the Bernanke Fed's 1.5 to 2 percent target could require double-digit interest rates, something "not seen since the days of Paul Volcker."[4] Looking further ahead, he says, "I fear that my successors on the FOMC, as they strive to maintain price stability in the coming quarter century, will run into populist resistance from Congress, if not from the White House."[5] If the Fed gives in to that pressure, inflation could average 4 to 5 percent by the year 2030. Hence he expects price losses for bondholders, a weak stock market, and low home price increases.

PLAYING THE HAND YOU'RE DEALT

In his first two years the Bernanke Fed did a slow 180-degree turn, starting out fighting inflation, shifting to neutral (balancing the risk of recession and financial market collapse against the risk of over-easing and inflation); and finally in January 2008, shifting to recession risk management. This policy turn amply demonstrates Bernanke's theories in action.

STAGE ONE: DEFENDING BOTH
BOUNDARIES OF THE INFLATION TARGET

When it became clear that Bernanke was replacing Greenspan, the first question investors asked was: "Is he an anti-inflation hawk or a dove?" My immediate answer to that question: it depends. As an advocate of flexible inflation targeting, Bernanke should be an anti-inflation hawk when inflation is above target, but an anti-deflation dove when either a serious recession threatens or inflation goes too low.

"Helicopter Ben"

When Bernanke assumed the chairmanship of the Fed, the bond market had its doubts about him. Traders remember him as "Helicopter Ben" because he argued in 2002–2003 that, in extremis, the Fed could combat deflation—a steady fall in consumer prices—by dropping money from a helicopter. Bernanke's dovish talk was not unique: in a June 3, 2003, speech Greenspan worried about corrosive deflation and considered a pre-emptive strike, or "firebreak" against deflation.[6] All this talk of deflation and super-easy policy created a strong impression in the bond market that a 50-basis-point cut was likely to be implemented at the June 2003 FOMC meeting, pushing bond yields down to their lowest level in forty-seven years. When the expected 50-basis-point cut failed to materialize, a correction occurred (figure 14-3).

FIGURE 14-3

Ten-year Treasury yield

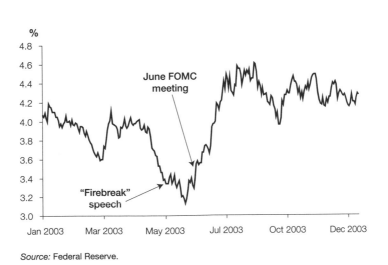

Source: Federal Reserve.

The Dreaded "D" Word

While the 2003 experience is burned into the psyche of bond traders, it tells us little about Bernanke's willingness to fight inflation. That spring, deflation, not inflation, was worrying the Fed. By June of that year, core CPI inflation had been flat for two months and had fallen from a peak year-on-year rate of 2.8 percent to 1.5 percent (figure 14-4). The economy had frozen in the run-up to the war in Iraq. The unemployment rate had moved back up to 6.4 percent, well above the 5 percent or so estimate of NAIRU. In a typical Phillips Curve model, inflation falls 0.6 percentage points per year for every percentage point of excess unemployment. By that calculation, absent a surge in growth, deflation was only a couple of years away. Little wonder that the May 2003 FOMC directive stated that "the probability of an unwelcome substantial fall in inflation, though minor, exceeds that of a pick-up in inflation."

FIGURE 14-4

Core CPI inflation

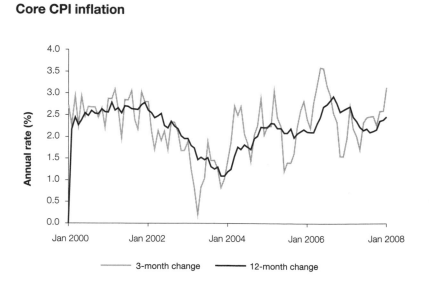

Source: Bureau of Labor Statistics.

Why worry so much about deflation? When prices are falling, consumers are encouraged to delay purchases until prices come down further. And if people don't spend, jobs are lost and prices fall even faster. Deflation also makes it hard for the central bank to stimulate the economy. When the Fed lowers interest rates, it hopes to convince people to borrow and spend. But if the prices of what people buy are falling fast enough, even a zero interest rate may not stimulate spending. Bernanke is one of the leading students of the Great Depression and Japan's "lost decade" of deflation. This background naturally dovetails with his view of inflation targeting—inflation can get too low as well as too high.

Falling prices were not the only thing worrying the Fed in 2003. With the funds rate down to 1.25 percent, a favorite refrain in the business press was that the Fed was running out of ammunition. Bernanke took up this public relations challenge, arguing that the Fed could go beyond cutting interest rates: "When inflation is already low and the fundamentals of the economy suddenly deteriorate, the central bank should act more preemptively and more aggressively than usual in cutting rates."[7] Bernanke understood that if the public begins to have doubts about the Fed's powers to revive the economy, those doubts can be self-fulfilling. One need look no further than Japan, with its recent "lost decade" of stagnant growth, falling prices, and impotent monetary policy. Bernanke wanted to make clear that the Fed had contingency plans to forestall such a disaster if it began to develop.

Now for Something Completely Different

But by the time Bernanke assumed the chairmanship, inflation—not deflation—was concentrating the minds of Fed officials. The big debate in the markets at the time was whether the Bernanke Fed would quickly move to the sidelines after Greenspan's fourteen rate hikes in a row. With inflation running above Bernanke's comfort zone and with the bond traders voicing doubts about Bernanke's anti-inflation credentials, would he encourage his committee to continue hiking rates? In the event, Bernanke played by the inflation targeting rule book, hiking rates by 25 basis points at each of his first three meetings.

STAGE TWO: LIMBO

At the July 2006 FOMC meeting, the Fed went on hold, while maintaining an anti-inflation policy bias. The directive from that meeting said: "The Committee judges that some inflation risks remain. The extent and timing of any additional firming that may be needed to address these risks will depend on the evolution of the outlook."[8] At the time this seemed like a brave move: on the morning of the meeting, the CPI report showed the third strong core inflation reading in a row. It seemed a little early for the Fed to be pausing in its tightening program. However, in the coming months, weak data suggested the policy pause was almost perfectly timed. Home construction started to fall sharply, and core measures of inflation stabilized. The Bernanke Fed seemed to have passed its second test.

The Fed remained in this limbo state for the next year, keeping the funds rate steady at 5.25 percent and repeatedly warning the markets that they saw a greater risk of inflation than of unacceptably low growth. The Fed remained on hold despite a deepening crisis in the housing market, falling construction, slowing home price inflation, and in early 2007 severe stress in the mortgage market. Why ignore the carnage? Fed officials noted that the rest of the economy and the rest of the financial markets were doing well. At the peak of the boom home construction was only 6 percent of GDP, so even with a sharp decline it was too small a part of the economy to cause a recession on its own. Similarly, subprime mortgages made up only 15 percent of the mortgage market and a much smaller fraction of capital markets, too small, it seemed, to hurt overall financial conditions significantly. Besides, the markets had become overextended in recent years, with unusually easy lending terms, so some adjustment was warranted. Also, overall consumer price inflation continued to run above Bernanke's comfort zone of 1 to 2 percent, and headline inflation was considerably higher.

STAGE THREE: RELUCTANT RATE CUTS

This limbo state ended abruptly in the summer of 2007. Each month thereafter a new element of the financial crisis was revealed: over the summer banks and hedge funds around the world reported major losses from subprime mortgages; in August the money market froze up as investors shunned commercial paper that was backed by mortgages; in September Northern Rock, a major bank, was rescued by the U.K. government; in October banks and investment banks reported major loses; in November the credit ratings of monolines (insurers of various debt obligations, including the debts of state and local governments) were brought into question; in November and December the market for interbank lending tightened up dramatically; in January and February 2008 the auction rate market (where state and local borrowing is rolled over) ran into serious trouble; and in March 2008 Bear Stearns, a major investment bank, was absorbed by JP Morgan Chase.

As the crisis developed the Bernanke Fed initially responded with Greenspan-style gradualism. In the fall of 2007, with the economy still growing and with some residual concerns about inflation, the Fed slowly cut rates. At the August 7 FOMC meeting the Fed stayed on hold and surprised the markets by retaining its anti-inflation bias. Then, ten days later, as the crisis in the capital markets intensified the Fed abruptly cut the discount rate by 50 basis points and hinted that if conditions didn't improve in the markets a cut in the funds rate could follow. The Fed then cut the funds rate 50 basis points at the September 18 meeting, 50 basis points at the October meeting, and 25 basis points again at the December meeting.

STAGE FOUR: RECESSION RISK
MANAGEMENT

In January 2008 gradualism came to an abrupt end, and Bernanke signaled a new period of recession risk management. The data flow had turned weaker, the press was full of confidence-sapping talk of recession, and capital markets were continuing to sell off. He first convened a special meeting of the FOMC on January 9 to gauge the "temperature of the room" before giving a speech hinting at more aggressive Fed action. According to the minutes, "Most participants were of the view that substantial additional policy easing in the near term might well be necessary."[9] A day later he gave a speech that ended gradualism, warning that recession, not inflation, was the main concern of the Fed: "In light of recent changes in the outlook for and the risks to growth, additional policy easing may well be necessary . . . we stand ready to take substantive additional action as needed to support growth and to provide adequate insurance against downside risks." And just in case the message wasn't clear, in the next and concluding paragraph, he repeated, "Financial and economic conditions can change quickly. Consequently, the Committee must remain exceptionally alert and flexible, prepared to act in a decisive and timely manner and, in particular, to counter any adverse dynamics that might threaten economic or financial stability."[10] On January 22, after a second conference call, the FOMC cut rates by 75 basis points and by another 50 basis points at the January 31 meeting.

This is the fastest policy change in the modern history of the Fed. The only time the Fed has moved the funds rates faster was when Volcker slammed on the brakes in 1979–1982 and essentially ignored the gyrations in the funds rate. Greenspan never moved rates more than 75 basis points in one move, let alone 125 basis points over a nine-day period.

The Fed not only embarked on unprecedented rate cuts, it also adopted an unprecedented array of new programs to directly add liquidity to the credit markets. This has lead to a bewildering array of new anachronisms including the Term Auction Facility (TAF), the Term Securities Lending Facility (TSLF), and the Primary Dealer Credit Facility (PDCF). This alphabet soup of new programs reflects attempts to extend existing policy tools and provide help to broader parts of the market.

Without getting into the complex institutional detail, there is a simple idea running through these programs.[11] The Fed owns a lot of liquid assets—that is, securities that are easy to trade and have virtually no risk of default, such as the debt of the U.S. government. The biggest chunk is in the Fed's System Open Market Account (SOMA), which had $790 bn at the start of the financial crisis in the summer of 2007. Meanwhile, in the markets many assets that normally are liquid—such as mortgage-related securities—had become very illiquid and hard to sell except at fire sale prices. Liquidity is the lifeblood of financial institutions and the Fed worried that panicky sales could cause a total freezing up of financial markets. If the markets freeze up, Fed attempts to revive the economy would be thwarted.

What the Fed has been doing is finding ways to lend or sell its liquid assets in exchange for illiquid assets (with safeguards against the risk of defaults). As this book goes to press the Fed had already committed $466 bn or more than half of its assets.[12] This helped cause a recovery in the markets in March and April 2008.

In addition, the Fed had created a new facility similar to the discount window—recall that this window is a way for the Fed to lend directly to banks. The new window is open to primary dealers.[13] The point of the discount window is to avoid bank runs. As in the movie *It's a Wonderful Life*, a bank run is a self-fulfilling panic. People pull their money out of a bank because they know that the bank can't pay every depositor immediately and if other depositors are pulling their money out you want to pull yours out first before the funds run dry. The modern equivalent of a bank run is when financial institutions stop lending to each other. Banks need to borrow regularly to fund their operations: if some institutions stop doing business with a distressed bank, then others will worry about their own loans and the distressed bank will quickly find it cannot borrow. Even if the distressed bank has a reasonably healthy balance sheet, a lending "strike" by other financial firms can cause bankruptcy. The Fed can stop this by opening up its own lending facility—the discount window. The simple promise that the Fed is there in a crisis can prevent the crisis from happening.

The question is: did the Bernanke Fed do the right thing?

15

Pressure Cooker

Bernanke's Performance in
His First Two Years

How has Ben Bernanke handled this tough economic environment? Let's turn to three common concerns about the Fed chairman. First, has he handled the economy and financial markets effectively—has he eased policy too much or too little? Second, why does such a strong proponent of transparency seem to have had so much trouble communicating? Third, is he or the Fed as an institution susceptible to political pressure?

DRAWN AND QUARTERED

As this book goes to press, the perfect storm of weak growth, rising inflation, and falling financial markets has unleashed a wave of criticism of the Fed. In one view, the Fed was cutting interest rates too much and losing its anti-inflation credibility. In another, the Fed had fallen hopelessly behind the curve in countering the negative shocks from the housing and credit markets and should have cut rates faster. And in some commentary, both of these criticisms are commingled. In other words, the Fed is being pulled in four directions at the same time: ease to help growth, ease to help markets, stay tight to stop inflation, stay tight to avoid moral hazard. Two almost diametrically opposite criticisms of the Fed emerged.

Alan Meltzer, an expert on Fed history, argues that the Fed had caved in to political and markets pressure when it cut rates dramatically in January 2008.[1] Editors at the *Wall Street Journal* wrote in January 2008, "Now we know what happens when Wall Street and the political class criticize Ben Bernanke for being 'behind the curve.' He gets in his race car and accelerates right through the curve. With yesterday's 50-basis-point cut, following last week's 75-point emergency reduction, we are certainly off to the monetary races."[2] A few weeks later, the *Journal* warned that oil, gold, and the euro—"the best indicators of inflation expectations"—are all hitting new highs.[3] Michael Darda, a business economist and frequent contributor to the *Wall Street Journal* op-ed page, maintained at the time, "We've literally forgotten that this is the very policy environment that led to the housing and mortgage problems in the first place . . . We're not going to see another housing bubble, but we could see more inflation."[4] Adam Posen, a political economist at the Peterson Institute for International Economics, agreed, saying the Fed's faster rate cuts would provide "too much rather than too little stimulus," pushing inflation noticeably higher.[5]

Another view is that the Fed has been too slow to cut rates in the face of a gathering storm in the housing and credit markets. In January 2008 Merrill Lynch economist David Rosenberg stated, "Bernanke is seriously behind the curve."[6] Robert Shiller, a professor of economics at Yale University who is famous for calling the 2000–2001 stock market crash, argued that "Bernanke did not see the magnitude of the housing recession. Volcker would have made a better job of it. He was an independent thinker and wasn't afraid."[7] Dean Baker of the Center for Economic and Policy Research wrote, "We are facing the worst financial meltdown since the Depression, and Mr. Bernanke was caught asleep at the wheel." He concludes, "There will be plenty of blame to go around in this

never been stress-tested, so there is no historical precedent for predicting where the financial firestorm will jump to next. Moreover, formal models of the economy are poorly equipped to handle a credit crisis. The financial accelerator effects that Bernanke wrote about—and many of us worry about—have proved very hard to model and are generally not included in formal statistical models of the economy. In many ways, the problems facing forecasters in 2007 and 2008 remind me of the early 1970s, when a new kind of economic shock—an oil crisis—confounded economic forecasts.

RISKY RISK MANAGEMENT

What about the opposite complaint: that the Fed eased too much, abandoned its role as a defender against inflation, and rewarded risk takers in the capital markets? It is always risky to make near-term predictions in the slow world of book publishing. Better to predict the Dow 36,000—some day—or the coming Great Depression—a few years from now. However, I will go out on a limb and argue that it made sense for the Fed to shift its focus to recession rather than inflation in early 2008. Indeed, prior to the Fed's shift, I had argued in my newsletter than the Fed needed to decide which war it was fighting—by cutting rates but sounding hawkish on inflation the Fed was undercutting the effectiveness of policy.[11] It seemed to me and my team at Lehman, even with Fed easing, that the economy was likely to remain quite weak and that inflation pressures would fade over time.

True, oil, gold, and the dollar all moved dramatically as the Fed eased policy, but they are all very noisy indicators of inflation expectations. I believe much of the run-up in oil and gold prices at the end of 2007 and in early 2008 reflected investors fleeing poor returns and high risks in other parts of the capital markets. With stock prices weak, credit markets frozen, and very low returns on cash-like investments, where were investors to turn? For many years, investors had abandoned commodities as an asset class, but after a five-year boom in prices many people in the portfolio advice business were recommending that commodities be part of diversified investment portfolios. Oil and gold prices are also sensitive to both supply disruptions and strong Asian demand. Much of the weakness in the dollar was due to concerns about a U.S. recession, a further decline in U.S. asset prices, and the threat of foreign central banks shifting out of dollars into other currencies. There may be an inflation signal in these indicators, but formal statistical tests show that none of them are reliable predictors of inflation.[12]

More direct measures of inflation expectations gave mixed signals. Perhaps the best measure of market expectations of inflation is *inflation breakevens*—a measure of how much inflation participants in the bond market anticipate.[13] Since inflation can bounce up and down a lot in the short term due to rising and falling energy prices, economists and policy makers often look at what the market is expecting for inflation several years ahead as a gauge of whether the market has faith that the Fed will control inflation over the long term. As figure 15-1 shows, investors have always had some doubts about the Fed holding inflation to 2 percent. However, inflation expectations have been relatively stable even as actual inflation has been bouncing up and down. At the time of this writing, this meas-

FIGURE 15-1

Inflation breakevens and consumer price inflation

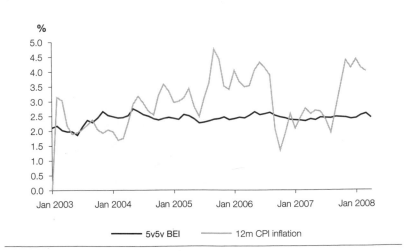

ure of expected inflation is in about the middle of its recent range. Other measures of inflation expectations were more stable. The Michigan survey of consumer expectations has moved up by a couple tenths in the last two years.[14] The Survey of Professional Forecasters shows stable expectations.[15] Finally, there is no sign that high headline inflation is bleeding into labor compensation. For example, the employment cost index has been growing at a stable 3.5 percent for the past six years. At the time of this writing, it appears that the Fed's anti-inflation credibility is fraying at the edges, but I believe that loss of confidence will be short-lived—I think the Fed was reasonable in assuming the economy and commodity markets would weaken, causing both actual and expected inflation to fall.

When the economy slows, it takes time for the unemployment rate and other measures of spare capacity to rise, taking the heat off of inflation. As figure 15-1 shows, inflation tends to peak in the middle of recessions and then falls sharply during the recession and into the recovery. If the economy is weak in 2008 and 2009, with the usual lags inflation fears should fade.

From the perspective of conservative economists a better criticism of the Bernanke Fed is not that it eased monetary policy too much, but that it was too aggressive in creating new programs to support the credit markets. I believe these programs were vital to preventing an even bigger capital markets crisis, helping reduce the risk of a major recession. However, these programs come with two costs. The first is moral hazard: by bailing out investors the Fed encourages risk taking in the markets. I believe the moral hazard cost is fairly low; after all, the Fed has stepped in only after very steep losses at financial firms, a big drop in stock prices, and considerable pain for both investors in securities and many of the people who took out exotic loans. The second cost is a likely increase in financial markets regulation: when financial bailouts occur, a quid pro quo of increased financial markets regulation often follows. Regulatory issues are beyond the scope of this book, but I believe the crazy quilt of financial markets regulation needs to be reworked. The issue is whether the new structure manages risk and consumer protection in a cost-efficient way that does not discourage financial innovation.

GREENSPAN'S GHOST

The Bernanke Fed should be judged relative to the challenges it faces and the tools it has to deal with those challenges. Bernanke inherited both an inflation problem and a capital markets crisis. The Fed cannot both raise rates to fight inflation and cut rates to help the economy and capital markets. It also cannot ease policy to save the economy without helping out risk takers in capital markets. Despite Alan Greenspan's outsized reputation, the Fed is neither an infallible forecasting institution nor does it have very precise control over the economy. On the margin, one could argue that the Fed erred in the balancing of these risks. On the one hand, perhaps the Fed should have been quicker to cut rates in 2007. On the other hand, perhaps the Fed was too abrupt or too aggressive in its policy moves in early 2008. However, these possible mistakes are well within the historic experience of central banking.

Every economic and financial disaster is predicted by *some*one; indeed, there are a number of economists who almost always see a recession just around the corner. Just as a stopped clock is right twice a day, these perma-bears are remarkably accurate on occasion. In the case of the housing bubble, the perma-bears called a housing collapse several times before it happened. The Fed could have taken the advice of the most bearish forecasters, but that would have meant easing back in 2006, stoking even more inflation pressure in 2007 and 2008. Moreover, if the Fed were to always focus on the most bearish forecasts, it will have a bias to keep rates too low, and runaway inflation would be inevitable. The economics consensus is often wrong, but the Fed shouldn't be criticized for doubting a scenario that is radically different than most economists expect.

THERE MUST BE SOME
MISUNDERSTANDING

Although his grades have slipped over time, polls of economists in his first two years have on average given Bernanke an overall grade of B, with an A for his actions but a C for his communication.[16] How is this possible? How could such a strong proponent of policy transparency and plain speaking have such a tough time communicating with the markets and Fed watchers? I believe the Bernanke Fed is partly to blame, but the markets should also share some of the blame for clinging to their Greenspan decoder rings too long. The Fed's more democratic decision-making process and a remarkably complicated market and economic environment have also contributed to the misunderstandings.

The Bartiromo Incident

Back in July 2006 Morgan Stanley's then-chief economist Stephen Roach argued that Bernanke was becoming a "serial flip-flopper." He wrote that unlike the European central banks that had been sending clear policy signals, Bernanke "has a rhetorical penchant for contradicting one statement after another."[17]

The alleged flip-flop that Roach was referring to, and perhaps the low point of Bernanke's rookie year, came in the spring of 2006. At the time the markets were on high alert for any signal of an end to the Fed's tightening cycle. In testimony to the Joint Economic Committee, Bernanke put on his professorial robes and gave a textbook description of how the Fed operates in the late stages of a tightening cycle. The Fed had already hiked rates significantly and, because it takes time for higher interest rates to cool the economy, there is always concern about overshooting—tightening too much. Bernanke stated, "Future policy actions will be increasingly dependent on the evolution of the economic outlook." Looking further ahead, he predicted that "at some point in the future the Committee may decide to take no action at one or more meetings in the interest of allowing more time to receive information relevant to the outlook. Of course, a decision to take no action at a particular meeting does not preclude action at subsequent meetings."[18]

The bond market reacted strongly to the speech: bond yields went down nine basis points on that day. According to one economist, quoted on MarketWatch, Bernanke's speech implied that

"June is now firmly penciled-in for a pause."[19] In my newsletter that week, I wrote that I hoped the pencil had an eraser because what Bernanke was trying to do was create more flexibility for policy, not a rigid promise.[20]

Sure enough, at a dinner with the press that weekend Bernanke revealed to CNBC reporter Maria Bartiromo that he was not signaling a pause but was signaling a need for "flexibility." Just to drive home the point, on June 5, after strong inflation data had been released, Bernanke described these stronger data as "unwelcome developments."[21] Bernanke seemed to have spun full circle: from hawk to dove and back to hawk.

There are two lessons from this incident: one for Bernanke and the other for investors. Bernanke learned that he has to be extremely careful around reporters. Greenspan had learned the same lesson when he appeared on *Meet the Press* early in his chairmanship and some ill-considered words caused a big move in the markets. That was the last time Greenspan appeared on such a program. After the Bartiromo incident, Bernanke told the Senate Banking Committee that he had had a "lapse of judgment" and that "in the future, [his] communications with the public and with the markets [would] be entirely through regular and formal channels."[22] Investors also learned a lesson: Bernanke has a very different communication style from Greenspan. When Greenspan made conditional statements, investors correctly read between the lines. If Greenspan said we "may pause at some point" it was reasonable to extrapolate that to mean "we are definitely pausing now." By contrast, with his more forthright speaking style, Bernanke should generally be taken at his word.

High Noon

Unfortunately, the Bartiromo incident was not the only communication problem the Bernanke Fed has had. In the western *High Noon*, Gary Cooper keeps changing his mind about whether to face a killer or leave town as his pacifist Quaker wife demands. In the end he sticks around and slays the villain.

Bernanke's high noon experience came with the credit crunch of 2007. During this period the Fed seemed to be constantly changing its mind:

- On August 7, after its regularly scheduled meeting, the FOMC announced it had retained its anti-inflation bias; a week later the Fed announced it was worried about growth and was cutting the discount rate.

- In the weeks leading up to the September FOMC meeting, a number of regional Fed presidents suggested that the FOMC was undecided about whether a rate cut was needed; in the event the Fed aggressively cut the funds rate by 50 basis points.

- In November, despite a major seizing up in the capital markets, FOMC members seemed to insist, in a string of speeches, that the Fed planned to pause at its December 11 meeting and would not cut the funds rate even if growth slowed; then suddenly, in the last week of November, both Bernanke and Vice Chairman Donald Kohn strongly suggested that the Fed would be considering a further rate cut on December 11.

- In January 2008, after following the gradualism playbook for many months, the FOMC suddenly cut 125 basis points, moving more than twice as much as was expected by both the markets and Fed watchers at the start of the month.

These seemingly sudden changes in direction have hurt Bernanke's reputation in the bond market. Is he a hawk or a dove? Is he being pushed around by the markets? Does he have command of the situation? These shifts stand in particular contrast to the "measured" tightening cycle that ended Greenspan's chairmanship, where every move was fully anticipated by the market by the time the meetings occurred. Why is Bernanke, such an advocate of transparency, so hard to pin down?

What We Seem to Have Here Is
a Failure to Communicate

There are a number of reasons for the Fed's apparent flip-flopping. Policy is inherently less predictable during periods of economic weakness than in times of economic expansion. Using a methodology developed by Ken Kuttner and Ben Bernanke, my colleague Kenji Abe and I estimated policy surprises from the Fed over the last eighteen years.[23] We found that in the early 1990s the average Fed rate move was up or down 32 basis points and typically half of the move was a surprise to the markets. By contrast, in the 2004–2006 tightening cycle, the markets almost perfectly anticipated all fourteen of the 25-basis-point rate hikes and all three 25-basis-point rate hikes made by the Greenspan and Bernanke Feds, respectively. Talk about transparency. By contrast, the recent moves made by the Bernanke Fed have been more like the early 1990s: on average about half of each move has been unanticipated.

Why is policy so hard to predict at some times and easy at others? A big part of the story is that tightening cycles are inherently more predictable because the Fed is trying to calibrate policy to a slow-moving problem: the risk of inflation. By contrast, easing cycles usually occur in an environment of rapidly changing economic and financial market risks. Indeed, Abe and I found that over the whole 1989 to 2007 period the Fed on average surprised the markets by 10 basis points during easing cycles and 3 basis points during tightening cycles.[24] In addition, there is a good case that the Greenspan Fed was a little too predictable in 2004 and 2005: perhaps if they had thrown in one or two 50-basis-point hikes they would have taken some of the air out of the housing and credit market bubbles.

The Bernanke Fed's communication problems also stem from two delicate balancing acts it is trying to perform. In the transition from overheated housing and credit markets to oversold markets, the Fed must balance the risk of easing too early—and bailing out investors—and easing too late—and allowing serious collateral damage to the economy. Like most central banks, the Fed welcomed the initial tightening of credit conditions in the summer of

FIGURE 15-2

Interest "spreads" for corporate borrowers

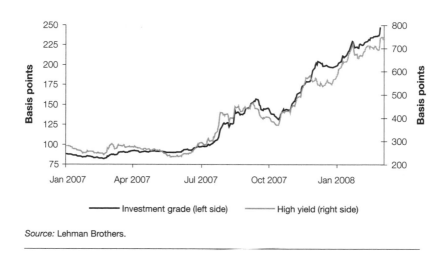

Source: Lehman Brothers.

2007 as a return to more normal risk pricing in the markets. Hence it stood aside and watched the markets sell off. However, it doesn't want to throw the baby out with the bathwater—to allow problems in capital markets to undercut the overall economy. So by mid-August it made the first of its abrupt turns, abandoning its anti-inflation focus and supplying liquidity into the markets to prevent serious damage to the economy.

The other balancing act is between recession and inflation risks. As the economy weakened in 2007, inflation accelerated. While the Fed can hope that weaker growth will cure the inflation problem, it needs to balance the risks. They are not simple to quantify: the Fed had to decide how deep the capital markets crisis would become, how much this would affect the economy, and how that growth reduction would translate into reduced inflation pressure. It is worth recalling that historically the Fed has had a tough time pulling off this balancing act. Typically, late in a business expansion inflation begins to run out of control and the Fed stomps on the brakes. The Fed tries to slow growth enough to curb inflation pressure but not enough to throw the economy into recession. Sometimes it works, but often another shock comes along and an already weak economy tumbles into recession.

A final reason for the Fed's communication missteps comes from Bernanke's efforts to reduce the cult of personality around the chairmanship and instill a more formal, more democratic decision process. The Fed normally meets only eight times a year, and in a rapidly shifting economic and financial environment the official policy directive can quickly get out of date. With a dominant chairman it is easier for the Fed to signal policy changes—the chairman simply makes a speech or calls up a reporter and drops the requisite coded message. However, a more democratic chairman, particularly one that eschews the spotlight, has to convene the committee to signal a change of path. In a complex economic environment, it is impossible for a democratic committee to telegraph policy changes in advance of meetings, because they themselves will not know the outcome until they have met and discussed the options.

War Powers

The markets had their doubts about Bernanke when he stepped into the job, and bouts of poor communication have lessened confidence in his leadership. In the fall of 2007, the Fed undercut its policy easings with verbal tightenings, repeatedly suggesting that with continued inflation risks, further easing was unlikely. The repeated references to inflation risks probably kept hawks on the committee happy, but confused the markets. Was the Fed really as worried about inflation as it was about weakness in the economy? If risks were balanced, why did the Fed keep cutting rates? Was it simply caving in to market or political pressures? The Bernanke Fed would have been better off sending a clearer, more consistent message—inflation is a concern, but downside risks to growth are a greater concern. If this provoked dissents from the FOMC hawks, so be it.

The Bernanke Fed has had serious communication problems, but Bernanke is learning to communicate with the markets more clearly and more frequently. In late November 2007 and again in early January 2008, both Bernanke and Vice Chairman Kohn gave speeches that "marked to market" the Fed's concerns, suggesting that the Fed understood the distress in the markets and that the old official directive no longer applied. Then in January, after consulting with his committee, Bernanke signaled a sustained switch to more aggressive easing. He also appears to have a made a more conscious effort to increase the visibility of himself and his trusted lieutenants. Democracy is a good thing, but in times of "war" quicker and more decisive decision making is needed.

FED INDEPENDENCE

Ben Bernanke's communication problems have been a hot topic in the markets, but a bigger long-run concern relates to the political independence of the Fed. Does Bernanke have the will, and does the Fed have the power, to resist political pressure in the years ahead? Without Greenspan's obvious political savvy, can any Fed chairman maintain the independence of the Fed?

Three leading economists have expressed concerns about the independence of the Fed. Back in 2005, Paul Krugman, a Princeton professor and *New York Times* columnist, argued that the loyalty demanded from a chairman of the Council of Economic Advisers (CEA) could undercut Bernanke's independence should he return to the Fed.[25] After all, over the years, the CEA job has become more political. Initially, the CEA was viewed as a quasi-academic think tank that helped develop policy ideas. However, in the mid-1970s, under Alan Greenspan, the CEA became increasingly tied to official administration policy, and the power structure of the group shifted from three roughly coequal partners to a chairman-dominated group. Consistent with this, in his own term at the CEA, Bernanke carefully parroted the party line, downplaying concerns about the imbalances in the economy such as the risk of a bubble in the housing market.

A more recent voice of concern comes from Alan Meltzer, a leading monetarist economist who is writing a book on the history of the Fed. In a February 2008 op-ed piece in the *Wall Street Journal*, he asks, "Is the Federal Reserve an independent monetary authority or a handmaiden beholden to political and market players? Has it reverted to its mistaken behavior in the 1970s?"[26] The answer, in Meltzer's view, is an emphatic yes: "Recent actions and public commitments, including Fed Chairman Ben Bernanke's testimony to Congress yesterday—where he warned of a steeper decline and suggested that more rate cuts lie ahead—leave little doubt on both counts."

Meltzer goes on to explain: "One lesson of the inflationary 1970s: A country that will not accept the possibility of a small recession will end up having a big one when the politicians at last respond to the public's complaints about inflation." He then points out that none of the major forecasting organizations—the International Monetary Fund, the Congressional Budget Office, and the FOMC itself—is forecasting a recession. He concludes by saying that the Fed's forecast of a small rise in the unemployment rate will do little to stop inflation: "The Fed should insist on its obligation to prevent inflation and sustain growth, not sacrificing inflation to lower unemployment before the election."

Greenspan has also expressed concerns, not about Bernanke in particular, but about the political vulnerability of the Fed as an institution. For a former Fed official like me, one of the most shocking parts of Greenspan's memoir is his prediction that the Fed could lose its independence in the near future. He envisions a nasty chain of events. He believes that inflation has been held down in recent years by a flood of cheap products from China and other newly liberalized economies. But that process is probably coming to an end. "So at some point in the next few years, unless contained," he predicts, "inflation will return to a higher long-term rate."[27] How high? He expects inflation to return to the 4 to 5 percent range of recent decades. He concludes that if the Fed wants to hold inflation in the 1 to 2 percent range, it "would have to constrain monetary expansion so drastically that it could temporarily drive up interest rates into the double-digit range not seen since the days of Paul Volcker."[28] Worse still, we could "see a return of populist, anti-Fed rhetoric, which has lain dormant since 1991."[29] In other words, rising prices for Chinese imports will unleash a sequence of events that could end with a loss of independence of the Federal Reserve (figure 15-3).

Greenspan concludes, "I regret to say that Federal Reserve independence is not set in stone. FOMC discretion is granted by statute and can be withdrawn by statute. I fear that my successors on the FOMC, as they strive to maintain price stability in the coming quarter century, will run into populist resistance from Congress, if not from the White House. As Fed chairman, I was largely spared such pressures because long-term interest rates, especially mortgage interest rates, declined persistently throughout my tenure."[30]

Surviving the School Board

I find none of these arguments convincing. Let's start with the easiest one: Krugman's point about the corrupting influence of the CEA. I think the CEA experience is largely irrelevant. Indeed, for this book I have quoted liberally from many Bernanke speeches,

FIGURE 15-3

Chinese import prices, 2004–2007

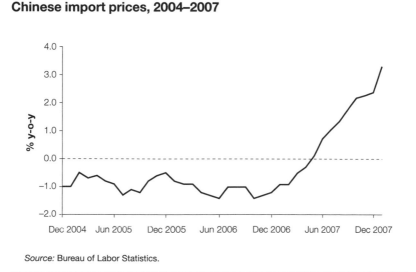

Source: Bureau of Labor Statistics.

but from none of his speeches while at the CEA. When, in early 2005, Bernanke was suggested as a possible replacement for Gregory Mankiw as chairman of the CEA I wrote in my weekly newsletter that he was probably taking the job to fill out an already strong résumé and as a way to improve his chances for landing the real plum job, the Fed chairmanship.[31] I argued that a few months at the White House do not overturn decades of independent research and several years of independent-minded service as a Fed governor. It is true that Bernanke stuck close to the party line at the CEA, but to do anything else would likely have caused the Bush administration to send him packing back to Princeton and ended his bid to be Fed chairman. As I wrote in 2005, "Bernanke has proved himself a strong, independent-minded economist at the Fed, and we would expect him to return to form if appointed chairman."[32]

Meltzer's view that Bernanke is being seduced by politicians also seems far-fetched.[33] In the political realm, Bernanke is the exact opposite of Greenspan. Greenspan was the consummate insider. By contrast, and by all accounts, Bernanke is remarkably nonpartisan. When his candidacy for the Fed chairmanship became clear, Fed watch reporters started to dig around for evidence of Bernanke's political partisanship. They came up with a dry well. For example, New York Times reporter Edmund Andrews concluded that Bernanke was so nonpartisan that "for years some of his closest friends did not know that [he] was a Republican."[34] Alan Blinder, who shared the same faculty room with Bernanke at Princeton (and is a former Fed governor), confirms this observation: "We wrote articles together and sat at the same lunch table thousands of times before I knew he was a Republican . . . We never talked politics."[35] On a similar note, longtime collaborator and NYU professor Mark Gertler says, "If you read anything he's written, you cannot figure out which political party he's associated with." More telling, Gertler argues, "He wants to be known as a great central banker. Those with the worst reputations are the ones who helped politicians."[36] As for political connections, as Bernanke himself admits, "The sum of my political experience consisted of two terms on the local school board, six grueling years during which my fellow board members and I were trashed alternately by angry parents and angry taxpayers."[37]

I believe Meltzer is taking the Fed and other official forecasts a little too literally. It is true that the FOMC's baseline forecast at the start of 2008 in no way justified aggressive rate cuts. However, remember where these forecasts came from. First, the Fed's forecasts assume appropriate monetary policy—in other words, they expect a moderate slowdown, but presumably only with further Fed easing. Second, the risks the Fed was talking about were quite high. The Fed's baseline looked very benign, with growth returning to trend in late 2008, but the alternative scenarios are quite ugly, including a possible major recession. Third, we should not be too swayed by the Fed's optimistic baseline. Bernanke has not laid out the gory details of the alternative scenarios because he knows such an alarmist presentation could be a self-fulfilling blow to investor and consumer confidence. Finally, as of this writing a quick return to healthy growth seemed unlikely. With home prices falling and foreclosures rising at an accelerating rate, and banks restraining credit as they adjust to losses on bad loans, it now seems that Fed rate cuts were needed just for the economy to run in place.

Taking Away the Car Keys

Greenspan's concern about populist pressure is, I think, a more realistic threat to Fed independence than either Krugman or Meltzer's concerns, but mainly as a long-run worry. Let's take a closer look at Greenspan's scenario. The nasty chain of events he is predicting starts with a rise in the price of goods from China. I don't buy it. The main drivers of inflation are economic slack in the medium term and the fortitude of the Fed in the long term. Cheap goods from China can help contain inflation, but in my job as an economic forecaster I worry a lot more about the 60 percent of consumer spending on domestically produced services than on the less than 3 percent of consumer spending on Chinese products (figure 15-4).[38] There is a growing economics literature on this topic, including several studies

FIGURE 15-4

U.S. PCE shares, 2006

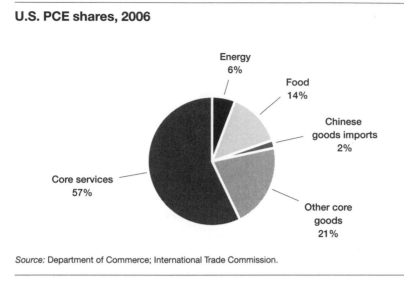

Energy
6%

Food
14%

Chinese
goods imports
2%

Core services
57%

Other core
goods
21%

Source: Department of Commerce; International Trade Commission.

from Greenspan's former employer.[39] The consensus is that global forces may have sliced a few tenths off of U.S. inflation, but domestic forces remain more important than global forces.

The upshot is that Bernanke may face a tougher challenge than Greenspan. This does not mean he will be forced to give in to inflation; it simply means that the Fed may need to offset loss of disinflation global pressure by allowing a slightly higher average unemployment rate. As Milton Friedman put it, "Inflation is always and everywhere a monetary phenomenon." Good monetary policy, not cheap goods from China, is the main reason inflation has been low since the early 1980s, and good monetary policy should be able to offset the inflationary pressures out of China.

Whatever the source of inflation pressure, Bernanke will likely work hard to avoid a situation where the Fed's independence is threatened. The 1970s experience is burned into the psyche of every senior Fed official, and it is widely understood that the Fed policy mistakes were central to this unfortunate episode. The 1970s Fed did not fully understand, or accept, the modern Phillips Curve model of inflation. Fed Chairman Arthur Burns seemed to blame everything except his own policies for the rise in inflation, and G. William Miller did not have the proper intellectual background for a Fed chairman. Moreover, within the 1970s experience, there is particular embarrassment over the way Burns, a close associate of the Nixon administration, eased monetary policy right before the 1972 presidential election.

Surely the Bernanke Fed understands the slippery slope nature of inflation. It is much better to nip inflation in the bud than to let it escalate and be forced ultimately into a Volcker-style battle. Moreover, while some aspects of the inflation backdrop have worsened, others have improved. Most important, years of low inflation have convinced most Americans to expect low inflation. As a result, there is a psychology of cost containment. Today, when the labor market is tight, workers are not as quick to demand wage increases, and when commodity and other costs rise, firms fight hard to offset the price pressures. Many of the things that made inflation so explosive in the 1970s—such as automatic cost of living increases in wage agreements—no longer obtain.

Bernanke should benefit from the increased independence of the Fed. As I have shown, the last two U.S. presidents carefully refrained from criticizing the Fed, and the pressure from Congress has declined over time as well. The last three macroeconomics appointments to the board have all been nonpolitical technocrats: Ben Bernanke, Donald Kohn, and Frederic Mishkin. Perhaps politicians have learned that having a competent, nonpolitical Fed chairman reduces the frequency of economic or financial accidents and is therefore good politics. Even in the early dark days of Paul Volcker's chairmanship, the Fed was able to retain its independence, and it had taken a decade of bad policy to create that dangerous situation. Surely those lessons didn't retire with Greenspan. As Bernanke puts it, since Paul Volcker vanquished inflation in the early 1980s, "monetary policy-makers, political leaders, and the public have been persuaded by two decades of experience that low and stable inflation has very substantial economic benefits."[40] The Fed will want to be careful in dissipating this hard-won political capital, and the best way to do that is to fight inflation before it gets out of hand.

Conclusion

Can He Walk the Walk?

The Outlook for the Bernanke Fed

R eading Ben Bernanke's speeches as a Fed governor is like staring at a stereogram—a three-dimensional picture that seems to rise up from the page. What stands out is that he seems to have systematically trained himself to become a top central banker. In almost fifty speeches, he covered not only most of the hot issues of monetary policy but also the regulatory and financial market issues. Moreover, he packed each speech with footnotes and references and carefully weighed all sides of the issues. As far as it is possible to study for the job, Bernanke has done it.

PAST PERFORMANCE IS NOT NECESSARILY INDICATIVE OF FUTURE RESULTS

There is one big caveat in my sanguine spin on Bernanke: a great student may not become a great practitioner. Consider Fed chair Arthur Burns in the 1970s. Burns had great training, including an impressive academic record, and extensive policy experience. Yet his chairmanship was a disaster. He started out arguing that monetary discipline was the key to containing inflation. Then he found one excuse after another to avoid administering the tough monetary medicine. His worst mistake was pushing for a disastrous policy of wage and price controls.[1] He invented the concept of a core measure of inflation, then excluded every high-inflation item from the core. Frequently, he found excuses to choose a policy path that the Nixon administration would favor. The job can make or break the man.

THE WINTER OF OUR DISCONTENT

A hot topic on weekend business shows in the spring of 2008 was whether the next president will reappoint Bernanke as Fed chairman when his four-year term expires in 2010. Two factors are driving this debate—first, that a new president, particularly a Democratic president, may want to choose his or her own person for such an important policy job; and second, that the economy and the financial markets have performed poorly during Bernanke's tenure and someone new might do a better job. None of the candidates have suggested they are looking for a change of leadership, but none have come out and given the kind of endorsements Greenspan got around recent elections.

Not surprisingly, I think that we ought not to bring politics into the reappointment decision. While Bernanke is a Republican, he is an unbiased technocrat when doing his job as Fed chairman. The recent tradition of keeping party politics out of the Fed has served the country well. Both Bill Clinton and George W. Bush had a hands-off policy towards the Fed. Moreover, if Republican President Reagan could reappoint the Democratic Chairman Paul Volcker and if Democratic President Bill Clinton could reappoint the Republican Alan Greenspan, then why should a Democratic president replace Bernanke?

A better reason to withhold reappointment would be if Bernanke is judged to be incompetent as chairman. However, dealt the same challenging environment, I doubt any of the other potential candidates for the job would have performed better. Recessions and financial panics are part of the normal cycles of the U.S. economy; both seem to recur every five or ten years. To the extent that the Fed deserves blame in the current cycle, it is Greenspan, not Bernanke, who laid the groundwork by letting inflation pressures build and by failing to curb the bubbles in the housing and credit markets.

Has the Bernanke Fed been asleep at the wheel? Only in a limited sense. At the start of the easing cycle the Fed moved more slowly than the markets were demanding, but, as I hope I have shown, the Fed was quicker to recognize the seriousness of the problems than most of the economics profession. The Bernanke Fed has been active by historic standards: for the two recessions he faced, Greenspan did not cut rates as quickly before the recession as Bernanke. Going further back, Fed chairmen historically did not start to cut until recessions were already under way. The Bernanke Fed also was not slow compared with the actions of fiscal policy: even with Bernanke's urging, fiscal ease was not agreed on until February 2008. Thus fiscal policy has lagged well behind monetary policy, with the agreement on a stimulus package coming six months after the Fed first cut the discount rate back in August 2007 and with the actual implementation of fiscal ease several months later. If Bernanke was asleep at the wheel, he woke up a lot faster than his fiscal policy peers.

INQUIRING MINDS WANT TO KNOW

What is the outlook for the Fed? When the storm clouds around the economy and financial markets clear, and assuming Bernanke is reappointed in 2010, I would expect further moves toward a flexible inflation target. The Bernanke Fed has already revealed—in a backdoor fashion—what Frederic Mishkin calls *mandate-consistent* inflation of 1.5 to 2.0 percent for the PCE deflator. This still leaves the Fed well behind the targeting regimes at other central banks. Next steps should include: (1) formally announcing a target—using euphemistic language such as "mandate-consistent" or "a price stability understanding" rather than the politically incorrect "target"; and (2) improving the quarterly forecast by having each member make consistent assumptions for monetary policy—probably assuming the funds rate follows what is priced into the markets. These would be major steps toward improved transparency.

I would also expect recent changes in Bernanke's leadership style to continue. This means continuing the democratic approach of encouraging an active debate at the Fed, but pushing policy ahead quickly even if it means regular dissents at meetings. It also means talking more to the markets. Bernanke has learned that, in a rapidly changing financial climate, the Fed's formal communication through policy directives is too slow. At some point, I would expect the Fed to scrap its strange meeting schedule—eight times per year at oddly spaced intervals—and switch to monthly meetings and perhaps regular intermeeting conference calls as well.

The rules of the game for Fed watchers—both professionals (like me) and budding students (likely my beloved readers)—are changing. In gauging likely Fed actions, investors should put more weight on the comments of the core members of the FOMC—Bernanke, Kohn, Mishkin, and Geithner—and less weight on dissenters from the regional banks. In keeping with Bernanke's financial accelerator framework, investors should also keep a very close eye on the evolution of key indicators of stress, including measures of imbalance in the housing market (inventory, foreclosure, and price trends) and in the credit markets (credit spreads and indicators of credit rationing such as the Fed's Senior Loan Officer Survey).

The policy debate at the Fed will likely remain quite open. Dissenting votes at FOMC meetings have already become more frequent under Bernanke than in the second half of Greenspan's chairmanship. Given the complicated and uncertain economic and financial environment ahead, no doubt there will be more dissents. However, in one sense these dissents are not as meaningful as they were under Greenspan. Under Greenspan dissents could sometimes be the tip of an iceberg of disagreement; under Bernanke there should be no hidden dissents.

I expect Bernanke's communication style to continue to evolve, particularly in his interactions with Congress. While the Fed chairman should try to clearly explain the Fed's goals, actions, and challenges, he should try to guide the discussion in productive ways. My colleague John Llewellyn argues that relative to Greenspan, Bernanke sometimes sounds like he is talking more to the economics profession rather than the general public. Bernanke also needs to learn to shape hostile and sometimes ill-informed questions into a sensible discussion about what the Fed can and can't do.

I would expect a major increase in Fed research on the interplay between capital markets and the economy. This research should include collecting more information from financial institutions and doing more analysis of the modern financial architecture. It also includes extension of Bernanke's work on the financial accelerator model. While deep discussion of it is beyond the scope of this book, there will also be a big push to have more data disclosure on obscure areas of the capital markets and changes in financial markets regulation, particularly around the mortgage industry.

One of the biggest challenges will be how the Fed exits from its policy of radical risk management. In response to the financial crisis, the Fed has instituted a very aggressive approach to lend liquid assets in exchange for illiquid assets. It has also pushed the funds rate to a very low level. When the markets and economy recover, the Fed leadership must avoid repeating Greenspan's mistake (in the early part of this decade) of pushing the funds rate to emergency lows during the crisis but then removing the easy policy at a "measured pace" when the crisis ended.

Finally, while most Fed officials are loath to admit it, they must be considering changes in the way they handle suspected asset bubbles. Gary Stern, veteran president of the Minneapolis Fed, notes that it is "neither easy nor costless to deal with the aftermath of unsustainable asset prices" and "it is well within the realm of possibility for policymakers to build support for and at least obtain tolerance of policies designed to address excesses."[2] In the past Bernanke has argued that bubbles are too hard to identify and stop for the Fed to take preemptive action. However, his earlier writings suggest that he understands, and has some sympathy for, the lean-against-the-bubble strategy. He notes, "According to this view, the Fed should try to gently steer asset prices away from a presumed bubble path. For example, seeing a rapid appreciation of stock prices, not only should the Fed tighten enough to offset the likely effects of the boom on inflation and output, but also it should add another 25 to 50 basis points for good measure, in the hope of discouraging increases in stock prices it judges to be excessive."[4] He compares this to taking out a little insurance, and notes that "it is rarely the case in economics that the optimal amount of insurance in any situation is zero."[5] I cannot imagine a Bernanke-led Fed turning its focus away from inflation and growth and fighting hard against a possible asset market bubble; but perhaps he would be more inclined to err quietly on the side of tighter policy in the face of a future asset bubble.

A CHALLENGING ENVIRONMENT

How will the economy fare in the years ahead? Will the Bernanke Fed be able to achieve the same growth performance as the Greenspan Fed? And will the Fed hold the line on inflation or—as Greenspan argues—will it ultimately submit to political pressure?

The Fed will likely face a very challenging economic environment in both the near term and the long term. Shocks to asset markets affect the economy with long and variable lags: hence, the popping of the credit and housing bubbles is likely to constrain the economy well into 2009. Fortunately, as Bernanke's writings on the Great Depression and the Japanese deflation point out, the Fed still has plenty of ammunition to battle these problems—and Bernanke is not afraid to use it. With legal changes the Fed can continue to expand its program of selling or lending liquid assets to the markets and taking in illiquid assets onto its balance sheet. If times get tough enough, the Fed can cut the funds rate to zero if necessary. Predicting the course of Fed policy is difficult, but one thing seems certain: the Bernanke Fed will not hesitate to use all of its weapons.

Over the longer term, the Fed will probably have to accept a lower trend growth in the economy. The trend or potential growth rate of the economy depends on the growth in the number of workers (the labor force) and the growth in output per hour (labor productivity). While the pace of technological innovation remains fast, the benefits to labor productivity growth are probably past their peak. For example, the early outsized productivity gains from the use of the Internet are unlikely to be repeated. Furthermore, the low U.S. savings rate has meant a lower rate of productivity-enhancing investment and more borrowing overseas. That debt will be serviced out of future income.

The aging of the baby boom generation also undercuts the nation's growth potential. As these workers retire and are replaced by a smaller cohort, the growth in the labor force will slow. These retirements may also indirectly hurt productivity. A surge in Social Security and Medicare payments will put tremendous pressure on the federal budget. This suggests a tough balancing act between controlling spending, raising taxes, and containing the budget deficit. There is no easy answer: a sharp rise in tax rates will undercut incentives to work and innovate and a sharp rise in the budget deficit will divert resources away from private investment. Either way, the growth in labor productivity will likely slow. The first boomer hits age sixty-five in 2011, so the demographic shock is no longer something we can worry about later.

In this environment, if the Fed wants to preserve low inflation, it will have to accept lower GDP growth and probably a somewhat higher average unemployment rate. Attempting to maintain the old growth trend will only mean ever tighter capacity, an unsustainably low unemployment rate, and higher inflation. While Greenspan's memoirs likely overstate the risks, political pressure on the Fed will increase.[6] Fortunately, that pressure is starting from a low base and Fed officials have learned from the policy mistakes of the 1970s. While Greenspan expects the Fed to ultimately cave in to the pressure (see chapter 15), I am more optimistic—I think he has overstated the challenge and underestimated the resolve of the group he left behind. A good early test of who is right will come in

2010 when the new president decides whether to reappoint a non-political technocrat (e.g., Bernanke), replace him with a similar candidate, or repeat the mistake of the 1970s and appoint a politically pliant person (e.g., Burns) or someone unqualified for the job (e.g., Miller).

"Fasten your seatbelts, it's going to be a bumpy night!"[7]

Notes

Acknowledgments

1. William Fleckenstein with Frederick Sheehan, *Greenspan's Bubbles: The Age of Ignorance at the Federal Reserve* (New York: McGraw-Hill, 2008).

2. Ethan Harris, "Bernanke: A Guide to the New Fed Chairman," *Lehman Brothers Global Economics*, February 10, 2006.

Chapter 1

1. Bob Woodward, *Maestro: Greenspan's Fed and the American Boom* (New York: Simon and Schuster, 2005).

2. *Time*, February 15, 1999.

3. Alan S. Blinder and Ricardo Reis, "Understanding the Greenspan Standard," speech at Federal Reserve Bank of Kansas City Symposium, Jackson Hole, WY, August 2005.

4. Ibid.

5. See, for example, Steve Schifferes, "Who Will Replace Greenspan?" BBC News, news.bbc.co.uk, October 12, 2005.

6. Ethan Harris, "After Greenspan," *Lehman Brothers Global Weekly Economic Monitor*, October 14, 2005.

7. John M. Berry, "Bernanke Gives Fed an Explicit Inflation Target," www.bloomberg.com, November 17, 2007.

8. Sheryl Gay Stolberg, "And in This Corner, Fed Choice Is Blip on Some Senator's Radar," *New York Times*, January 31, 2006.

Chapter 2

1. See Robert H. Frank and Ben S. Bernanke, *Principles of Economics*, 3rd edition (Boston: McGraw-Hill/Irwin, 2007), 536–540.

2. See Charles Bean, "Is There a New Consensus in Monetary Policy?" in *Is There a New Consensus in Macroeconomics?* ed. Philip Arestis (New York: Palgrave Macmillan, 2007).

3. The original paper focused on the relationship between wages and un-employment. See A. W. Phillips, "The Relation Between Unemployment and the Rate of Change of Money Wage Rates in the United Kingdom, 1861–1957," *Economica*, November 1958, 183–299.

4. Milton Friedman, "The Role of Monetary Policy," *American Economic Review*, March 1968, 1–17; Edmund Phelps, "Money Wage Dynamics and Labor Market Equilibrium," in *Microeconomic Foundations of Employment and Inflation Theory*, ed. Edmund Phelps (New York: W.W. Norton, 1970), 124–166.

5. Andrew B. Abel and Ben S. Bernanke, *Macroeconomics*, 5th edition (Boston: Pearson/Addison-Wesley, 2005).

6. For a summary see Joseph Abate, "Transmission Effects," *Lehman Brothers Global Weekly Economic Monitor*, January 27, 2006; and Joseph Abate "Housing and the Credit Channel," *Lehman Brothers Global Weekly Economic Monitor*, February 3, 2006. For Bernanke's latest thoughts on this topic, see "The Financial Accelerator and the Credit Channel," speech at conference "Credit Channel of Monetary Policy in the Twenty-first Century," Federal Reserve Bank of Atlanta, Atlanta, GA, June 15, 2007.

7. Frederic S. Mishkin, "Housing and the Monetary Transmission Mechanism," Finance and Economics Discussion Series working paper, delivered at the Federal Reserve Bank of Kansas City's Economic Symposium, Jackson Hole, WY, August 2007; Frederic S. Mishkin, "Outlook and Risks for the U.S. Economy," speech to the Money Marketeers of New York University, New York, NY, September 10, 2007.

8. Ben S. Bernanke, "The Financial Accelerator and the Credit Channel," 3. By *pro-cyclical*, he means credit conditions tend to amplify the normal business cycle.

9. Kosuki Aoki, James Proudman, and Gertjan Vlieghe, "House Prices, Consumption, and Monetary Policy: A Financial Accelerator Approach," *Journal of Financial Intermediation* 13, October 2004, 414–435.

10. Check it out on Youtube: http://www.youtube.com/watch?v= SWksEJQEYVU.

11. Damian Paletta, "Fed Chief Lends His Ear to a Diverse Group" *New York Times*, February 7, 2008.

Chapter 3

1. William Greider, *The Secrets of the Temple* (New York: Simon & Schuster, 1989), 12.

2. An exception that proves the rule: G. William Miller's brief chairmanship from 1978 to 1979. Without experience in economics and monetary policy, he commanded little respect from the Committee. Miller "let the committee members vote as they wanted, without much guidance or influence

from the chairman" (Bob Woodward, *Maestro: Greenspan's Fed and the American Boom* [New York: Simon and Schuster, 2005], 107).

3. Setting the discount rate is an elaborate Kabuki dance. The boards of directors of each of the twelve Reserve Banks periodically meet to decide whether to request a discount rate change. The Board of Governors in Washington cannot act unless it has at least one request, but it can ignore requests. If a majority of the governors decides to change the discount rate, then the rate initially applies only to the requesting banks. Others quickly fall into line after emergency meetings of their boards. In practice, boards almost always coordinate changes with any change in the fed funds rate. This elaborate process inevitably spawns rumors about secret dissents at the Fed if one or another bank is slow to change the discount rate.

4. Alan Greenspan, "The Economic Outlook," testimony before the Joint Economic Committee, U.S. Congress, June 9, 2005.

5. Andrew B. Abel and Ben S. Bernanke *Macroeconomics*, 5th edition (Boston: Pearson/Addison Wesley, 2005), 543.

6. Ben S. Bernanke, "Oil and the Economy," remarks at the Distinguished Lecture Series, Darton College, October 21, 2004.

Chapter 4

1. William Greider, *The Secrets of the Temple* (New York: Simon & Schuster, 1989), 12.

2. Notable examples include the next three biggest economies, the EU, Japan, and the United Kingdom.

3. The original paper was Ray C. Fair, "The Effect of Economic Events on Votes for President," *The Review of Economics and Statistics*, May 1978, 159–173. His model is updated at: http://fairmodel.econ.yale.edu/vote2008/index2.htm.

4. Greider, *Secrets of the Temple*, 12.

5. In theory, a chairman could be denied reappointment to the chair and remain a regular governor. In his memoirs, Alan Greenspan writes that during one delayed reappointment decision he contemplated accepting such a demotion (Alan Greenspan, *The Age of Turbulence: Adventures in a New World* [New York: Penguin Press, 2007]).

6. Robert H. Frank and Ben S. Bernanke, *Principles of Economics*, 3rd edition (Boston: McGraw-Hill/Irwin, 2007), 845.

7. Greenspan, *Age of Turbulence*, 122.

8. Greider, *Secrets of the Temple*, 713.

9. Ibid., 48.

10. Greenspan, *Age of Turbulence*, 479.

11. Ibid.

12. Justin Martin, *Greenspan: The Man Behind the Money* (Cambridge, MA: Perseus Publishing, 2001), 185.

13. Greenspan, *Age of Turbulence*, 113.

14. Ibid., 119.

15. Martin, *Greenspan*, 196.

16. Bob Woodward, *Maestro: Greenspan's Fed and the American Boom*, (New York: Simon and Schuster, 2005), 91.

17. Steven Greenhouse, "Split Over Rates Ends Clinton-Fed Honeymoon" *New York Times*, December 20, 1993.

18. Ibid.

19. Greenspan, *Age of Turbulence*, 153.

20. Ibid., 207.

Chapter 5

1. Andrew Boyle, *Montagu Norman* (London: Cassell, 1967), 327.

2. Mervyn King, Deputy Governor's address to the joint luncheon of the American Economic Association and the American Finance Association, January 7, 2000.

3. William Greider, *The Secrets of the Temple* (New York: Simon & Schuster, 1989), 70.

4. Ibid., 181.

5. Ibid., 356.

6. Bob Woodward, *Maestro: Greenspan's Fed and the American Boom*, (New York: Simon and Schuster, 2005) 55.

7. Laurence H. Meyer, *A Term at the Fed: An Insider's View* (New York: HarperBusiness, 2004), 138.

8. Daniel Kadlec, "5 Ways the New Fed Chairman Will Be Different," *Time*, October 30, 2005; ibid.; Justin Martin, *Greenspan: The Man Behind the Money* (Cambridge, MA: Perseus Publishing 2000), 222; ibid.

9. Ben S. Bernanke, "Federal Reserve Communications," speech at the Cato Institute 25th Annual Monetary Conference, Washington, D.C., November 14, 2007.

10. Thomas Mayer, James S. Duesenberry, and Robert Z. Aliber, *Money, Banking and the Economy* (New York: W.W. Norton, 1981), 187.

11. Martin, *Greenspan*, 159.

12. Andrew Ferguson, "Alan Shrugged . . . and Washington Fell to Its Knees," *Weekly Standard*, October 8, 2007.

13. Alan Greenspan, *The Age of Turbulence: Adventures in a New World* (New York: Penguin Press, 2007), 151.

14. Ibid.

14. Woodward, *Maestro*, 137.

15. Ibid., 148.

16. Federal Open Market Committee transcripts, November 2000, www.federalreserve.gov.

17. Greg Ip, "The Enigma of Alan Greenspan," speech at Washington & Lee University, February 7, 2006.

18. Justin Martin, *Greenspan: The Man Behind the Money* (Cambridge, MA: Perseus Publishing 2000), 195.

19. Ip, "The Enigma of Alan Greenspan."

20. Louis Uchitelle, "Forecasts: Greenspan's Grades," *New York Times*, July 24, 1987.

21. Woodward, *Maestro*, 137.

22. Meyer, *A Term at the Fed*, 53.

23. Ibid., 60.

24. Blinder and Reis, "Understanding the Greenspan Standard," 79–80.

25. In a speech in the summer of 2005, then-new Dallas Fed President Richard Fisher said the Fed was in the "eighth inning" of its tightening cycle, suggesting one more rate hike to come. Like most Street economists, we were skeptical and titled our weekly newsletter "Extra Innings." The Fed ultimately raised the rate seventeen times.

26. Alan Greenspan, "State of the Economy," presentation before the Committee on Ways and Means, U.S. House of Representatives, January 20, 1999, www.federalreserve.gov.

27. Alan Greenspan "Monetary Policy and the Economic Outlook," testimony before the Joint Economic Committee, U. S. Congress, June 17, 1999.

28. Alan Greenspan, "The Federal Reserve's semiannual report on the economy and monetary policy," testimony before the Committee on Banking and Financial Services, U.S. House of Representatives, February 17, 2000.

29. Alan Greenspan, "The Economic Outlook," testimony before the Joint Economic Committee, U.S. Congress, June 9, 2005.

30. Ethan Harris and Joseph Abate, "Compensation Concerns" *Lehman Brothers Global Weekly Economic Monitor*, June 10, 2005.

31. In February 2004 Greenspan suggested that more homeowners should consider switching to adjustable rate mortgages (ARMs), where the interest rate rises and falls with short-term market interest rates. He pointed to a Federal Reserve staff study that showed homeowners with ARMs had saved money relative to those with conventional fixed rate mortgages over the last decade. But this advice came right at the low point for short-term interest rates: only a few months after Greenspan's speech, the Fed started its long interest rate hike cycle.

Chapter 8

1. For more on this topic see John Shin, "Targets, Not Targeting," *Lehman Brothers Global Weekly Economic Monitor*, April 22, 2005.

2. Finn Kydland and Edward Prescott, "Rules Rather than Discretion: The Inconsistency of Optimal Plans," *Journal of Political Economy* 85, June 1977, 473–492.

3. Ben S. Bernanke, "What Have We Learned Since October 1979?" remarks on panel discussion at the conference, "Reflections on Monetary Policy 25 Years After October 1979," St. Louis, MO, October 8, 2004.

4. Quoted in David Dodge, "70 Years of Central Banking in Canada," remarks to the Canadian Economics Association, Bank of Canada Review, Winter 2005–2006, www.bankofCanada.com. The failure of the money targets does not mean the monetarist school of thought, led by Milton Friedman, was a failure. While the monetarists' specific tactical recommendation—maintain a fixed growth in the money supply—did not work, their strategic recommendation of focusing monetary policy on controlling inflation has been adopted at almost all central banks. For more on the fading importance of money supply in Fed policy, see "Fedpoint: The Money Supply," http://www.newyorkfed.org/aboutthefed/fedpoint/fed49.html.

5. Bob Woodward, *Maestro: Greenspan's Fed and the American Boom* (New York: Simon and Schuster, 2005), 170.

6. Donald L. Kohn, remarks at the 28th annual policy conference, "Inflation Targeting: Prospects and Problems," Federal Reserve Bank of St. Louis, St. Louis, MO, October 17, 2003.

7. Alan S. Blinder and Ricardo Reis, "Understanding the Greenspan Standard," speech at the Federal Reserve Bank of Kansas City Symposium, Jackson Hole, WY, August 2005, 5.

8. Alan Greenspan, *The Age of Turbulence: Adventures in a New World* (New York: Penguin Press, 2007), 481.

9. Ibid., 481.

10. Ibid.

11. Ibid., 482.

12. Ben S. Bernanke et al., *Inflation Targeting: Lessons from the International Experience*, (Princeton, NJ: Princeton University Press, 1999); Ben S. Bernanke and Michael Woodford, eds., *The Inflation-Targeting Debate* (Chicago: University of Chicago Press, 2005).

13. There are many examples of this kind of discrepancy. In July 2007 the FOMC announced that its forecast for core PCE inflation from Q4 2006 to Q4 2007 was 2.0 to 2.25 percent. Bernanke testified that the Committee expected core inflation to "edge a bit lower, on net, over the remainder of this year." (Ben S. Bernanke "Semiannual Monetary Policy Report to the Con-

gress" before the Committee on Financial Services, U.S. House of Representatives, July 18, 2007.) However, core inflation had averaged an annualized 1.9 percent in the first half of 2007, so that the FOMC forecast could only be achieved if core inflation *accelerated to 2.1 to 2.6 percent* in the second half of the year. This failure to account for the first half base effect is among the easiest forecast errors to spot.

14. Quoted in Ben S. Bernanke et al., "Missing the Mark: The Truth About Inflation Targeting," *Foreign Affairs*, vol. 78, no. 5, September–October 1999, www.foreignaffairs.

15. Ben S. Bernanke, remarks at the 28th annual policy conference, "Inflation Targeting: Prospects and Problems," Federal Reserve Bank of St. Louis, October 17, 2003

16. See Ethan Harris and Zach Pandl, "Greenspan, Globalization and Inflation," *Lehman Brothers Global Weekly Economic Monitor*, October 12, 2007; and Ethan Harris, "Inflated Fears," *Lehman Brothers Global Weekly Economic Monitor*, September 28, 2007.

17. Even if the general public misses this subtle signal, FOMC members do not. They have implicitly agreed on an appropriate goal for inflation, thereby framing their discussion around appropriate policy responses when inflation exceeds this range.

18. Frederic S. Mishkin, "The Federal Reserve's Enhanced Communication Strategy and the Science of Monetary Policy," speech to the Undergraduate Economics Association, Massachusetts Institute of Technology, Cambridge, MA, November 29, 2007.

19. Federal Open Market Committee transcripts, July 1996, www.federalreserve.gov.

20. Ibid.

21. Krishna Guha, "Fed Chief Warned on Inflation Target" *Financial Times*, February 19, 2007.

Chapter 9

1. This chapter draws on John Shin's discussion of Bernanke's views on the Great Depression in Ethan Harris et al., "Bernanke: A Guide to the New Fed Chairman," *Lehman Brothers Weekly Global Economic Monitor*, February 10, 2006, 21–22.

2. Ben S. Bernanke, *Essays on the Great Depression* (Princeton, NJ: Princeton University Press, 2000), vii.

3. Ben S. Bernanke, "Deflation: Making Sure 'It' Doesn't Happen Here," remarks before the National Economists Club, Washington, DC, November 21, 2002.

4. Ibid.

5. Ibid.

6. Ibid.

7. Milton Friedman and Anna Jacobson Schwartz, *A Monetary History of the United States, 1867–1960* (Princeton, NJ: Princeton University Press, 1963).

8. Ben S. Bernanke, remarks at conference honoring Milton Friedman, University of Chicago, November 8, 2002.

9. Ben S. Bernanke, "Money, Gold and the Great Depression," Parker Willis Lecture in Economic Policy, Washington and Lee University, March 2, 2004.

10. Alan Greenspan, *The Age of Turbulence: Adventures in a New World* (New York: Penguin Press, 2007).

11. Bernanke, *Essays on the Great Depression*, viii.

12. Ibid.

13. Ibid.

14. Ben S. Bernanke, "Some Thoughts on Monetary Policy in Japan," speech before the Japan Society of Monetary Economics, May 31, 2003. Of course the speech had a caveat—"the opinions I give today are strictly my own"—but he was probably representing the majority view at the Fed.

15. Ibid.

16. Ibid.

17. Ibid.

18. Ibid.

19. Bernanke, "Deflation."

20. Ibid.

Chapter 10

1. Greg Ip, "Search for Fed Chairman Widens," *Wall Street Journal*, August 4, 2005.

2. Ben S. Bernanke "The Transition from Academic to Policy Maker," remarks at the Annual Meeting of the American Economic Association, Philadelphia, PA, January 7, 2005.

3. Ibid.

4. Bob Woodward, *Maestro: Greenspan's Fed and the American Boom* (New York: Simon and Schuster, 2005), 22.

5. Ben S. Bernanke, "Housing, Housing Finance, and Monetary Policy," speech at the Federal Reserve Bank of Kansas City's Economic Symposium, Jackson Hole, WY, August 31, 2007.

6. Alan S. Blinder and Ricardo Reis, "Understanding the Greenspan Standard," speech at the Federal Reserve Bank of Kansas City Symposium, Jackson Hole, WY, August 2005.

7. Congress is often quite slow to approve governors, so frequently there are one or two unfilled slots.

8. For a detailed discussion of the Fed's 1994 tightening cycle, see Ethan Harris and Melinda Mraz, "Fed Up: Lessons From 1994," *Lehman Brothers Global Weekly Economic Monitor*, June 28, 2004.

9. Federal Open Market Committee transcripts, February 1994, www.federalreserve.gov.

10. Ibid.

11. Laurence H. Meyer, *A Term at the Fed: An Insider's View* (New York: HarperBusiness, 2004), 53.

12. Vincent R. Reinhart, "The Governance, Communication, and Conduct of the Federal Reserve's Monetary Policy," speech at the U.S. Monetary Policy Forum, New York, February 29, 2008.

13. Ben S. Bernanke, Frederic S. Mishkin, and Adam S. Posen, "What Happens When Greenspan Is Gone?" *Wall Street Journal*, January 5, 2000.

14. Greg Ip, "Fed Chief Aims to Soften the Impact of His Words," *Wall Street Journal*, September 11, 2006. Ip says members signal a desire to speak out of turn by raising two hands.

15. Ben S. Bernanke, "Federal Reserve Communications," speech at the Cato Institute 25th Annual Monetary Conference, Washington, DC, November 14, 2007.

16. Richard W. Fisher, "The U.S., Mexican, and Border Economies," remarks before a Federal Reserve Bank of Dallas community luncheon, Dallas, TX, September 10, 2007.

17. Charles I. Plosser, "Two Pillars of Central Banking: Monetary Policy and Financial Stability," opening remarks to the Pennsylvania Association of Community Bankers, Waikoloa, HI, September 8, 2007.

18. Jeffrey M. Lacker, "The Economic Outlook" speech to the Charlotte Risk Management Association, Charlotte, NC, August 21, 2007.

19. Ben S. Bernanke, "National and Regional Economic Overview," speech at the presentation of the Citizen of the Carolinas Award, Charlotte, NC, November 29, 2007.

Chapter 11

1. Ben S. Bernanke, "Fedspeak," speech at the Meetings of the American Economic Association, San Diego, CA, January 3, 2004.

2. Ben. S. Bernanke, "Federal Reserve Communications," speech at the Cato Institute, 25th Annual Monetary Conference, Washington, DC, November 14, 2007.

3. Ibid.

4. Alan S. Blinder and Ricardo Reis, "Understanding the Greenspan Standard," presentation at the Federal Reserve Bank of Kansas City Symposium, Jackson Hole, WY, August 2005.

Chapter 12

1. See, for example, Joseph T. Abate, "To Pop or Not," *Lehman Brothers Global Weekly Economic Monitor*, June 24, 2005.

2. A "put" contract allows the buyer to sell an asset at a specified price. This protects the owner of the asset from a big price drop because the owner has the option to sell at the agreed price.

3. Alan Greenspan, "Economic Volatility," remarks at a symposium sponsored by the Federal Reserve Bank of Kansas City in Jackson Hole, WY, August 30, 2002.

4. Laurence H. Meyer, *A Term at the Fed: An Insider's View* (New York: HarperBusiness, 2004), 181.

5. Ben S. Bernanke, "Asset Prices Bubbles and Monetary Policy," remarks before the New York Chapter of the National Association of Business Economists, New York, October 15, 2002.

6. Donald L. Kohn, "Success and Failure of Monetary Policy since the 1950s," speech at "Monetary Policy Over Fifty Years," a conference to mark the fiftieth anniversary of the Deutsche Bundesbank, Frankfort, Germany, September 21, 2007.

7. Bernanke, "Asset Prices Bubbles and Monetary Policy."

8. Ibid.

9. Ibid.

10. Mark Gertler and Ben S. Bernanke, "Monetary Policy and Asset Price Volatility," remarks at conference, "New Challenges for Monetary Policy," Federal Reserve Bank of Kansas City, Jackson Hole, WY, August 1999.

11. Joseph Abate, "Housing Outlook," *Lehman Brothers Global Weekly Economic Monitor*, January 24, 2003.

12. Ethan Harris, "Favorable Feedback," *Lehman Brothers Global Weekly Economic Monitor*, July 15, 2005.

13. Alan Greenspan, The Federal Reserve Board's semiannual Monetary Policy Report to the Committee on Financial Services, U.S. House of Representatives, July 20, 2005.

14. Krishna Guha, "Greenspan Alert on U.S. House Prices," *Financial Times*, September 16, 2007.

15. John B. Taylor, "Housing and Monetary Policy," speech to the Symposium on Housing, Finance, and Monetary Policy sponsored by the Federal Reserve Bank of Kansas City, Jackson Hole, WY, September 2007.

16. Alan Greenspan, "The Fed Is Blameless on the Property Bubble," *Financial Times*, April 7, 2008.

17. Herbert Hoover, *The Memoirs of Herbert Hoover*, vol. 3 (New York: Macmillan and Co., 1952), 30.

Chapter 13

1. Ben S. Bernanke, "Gradualism," remarks at an economics luncheon cosponsored by the Federal Reserve Bank of San Francisco and the University of Washington, Seattle, WA, May 20, 2004.

2. Ibid.

3. Ben S. Bernanke, "Monetary Policy under Uncertainty," speech at the 32nd Annual Economic Policy Conference, Federal Reserve Bank of St. Louis, St. Louis, MO, October 19, 2007.

4. Ibid.

Part IV

1. Phil Izzo, "Bernanke's Ratings Slip, Despite Effort to Reignite Growth," *Wall Street Journal*, February 6, 2008.

Chapter 14

1. U.S. Economic Forecasts, Bloomberg Monthly survey, Bloomberg Finance L.P., February 9, 2006.

2. "British Banker Criticizes Greenspan's Public Comments," *International Herald Tribune*, May 16, 2007.

3. Mary Bruce, "Greenspan: U.S. Moving Closer to Recession," ABC News, www.abcnews.go.com, December 16, 2007.

4. Alan Greenspan, *The Age of Turbulence: Adventures in a New World* (New York: Penguin Press, 2007), 483.

5. Ibid., 478–479.

6. "Greenspan Sees U.S. Economic Pick-up, Rates On Hold," Bloomberg, June 3, 2003.

7. Ben S. Bernanke, "Deflation: Making Sure 'It' Doesn't Happen Here," remarks before the National Economics Club, Washington, DC, November 21, 2002.

8. Directive of the Federal Open Market Committee, May 2003, www.federalreserve.gov.

9. Included in the minutes of the Federal Open Market Committee, January 29–30, 2008, www.federalreserve.gov.

10. Ben S. Bernanke, "Financial Markets, the Economic Outlook, and Monetary Policy," speech delivered at the Women in Housing and Finance and Exchequer Club joint luncheon, Washington, DC, January 10, 2008.

11. For a description of the new programs visit the Web site of the Federal Reserve Bank of New York at www.newyorkfed.org/markets/Forms_of_Fed_Lending.pdf.

12. Author's calculation based on announced sizes of term auction facility (TAF), term securities lending facility (TSLF), and term repurchase agreement programs as of May 2008, plus total outstanding credit at the Primary Dealer Credit Facility (PDCF) on May 7, 2008.

13. Primary dealers are banks or investment banks who are allowed to trade directly with the Fed. They participate in auctions for new U.S. Treasury securities and they are required to make bids or offers when the Fed conducts open market operations. My company, Lehman Brothers, is one of twenty broker dealers.

Chapter 15

1. Allan H. Meltzer, "That '70s Show," *Wall Street Journal*, February 28, 2008.

2. "Nascar Bernanke," *Wall Street Journal*, January 31, 2008.

3. "The Bernanke Reflation," *Wall Street Journal*, February 29, 2008.

4. Quoted in Edmund L. Andrews, "Some Critics Say the Fed May Risk Repeating Earlier Mistakes," *New York Times*, January 24, 2008.

5. Ibid.

6. Roger Lowenstein "The Education of Ben Bernanke," *New York Times*, January 20, 2008.

7. Suzy Jagger, "Ben Bernanke Under Fire Ahead of Fed Rate Meeting," *The Times* (London), January 29, 2008.

8. Dean Baker, "Does Ben Bernanke Have to Go?" *Truthout | Perspective*, Center for Economic and Policy Research, February 18, 2008.

9. U.S. Economic Forecasts: Bloomberg Monthly Survey, Bloomberg Finance L.P., December 11, 2007.

10. The crisis is concentrated in areas of the capital markets that only narrow specialists understand. Economists, strategists, and central bankers have been scrambling to learn an alphabet soup of new markets and financial products—ABCP (asset-backed commercial paper), ABS (asset-backed securities), Alt-A (classification of mortgages), CDO (collateralized debt obligation), CDS (credit default swap), CLOs (collateralized loan obligation), CMBS (commercial mortgage-backed securities), SIV (structured investment vehicle), and so forth.

11. Ethan Harris, "Once More with a Feeling," *Lehman Brothers Global Weekly Economic Monitor*, December 14, 2007.

12. A number of studies have found that commodities such as oil and gold were useful predictors of future inflation until the early 1980s, but have

been poor predictors since. See, for example, S. Brock Blomberg and Ethan S. Harris, "The Commodity-Consumer Price Connection: Fact or Fable?" *Economic Policy Review*, Federal Reserve Bank of New York (October 2005), 21–38.

13. The breakevens are calculated as follows. The Treasury issues two kinds of bonds—a nominal bond that pays interest and an inflation-protected bond that pays interest and an additional amount based on how fast consumer price inflation is. The difference in the interest rate on these bonds is a gauge of how much inflation investors in these securities are expecting. For example, if a nominal five-year bond pays 5 percent interest and a five-year inflation-protected bond pays 3 percent interest than investors are signaling that on average they expect about 2 percent inflation over the next five years. In practice, there are a number of technical issues with this measure of inflation—there are a variety of risk premiums and liquidity premiums that can distort the inflation signal—but policy makers still look to it as a rough gauge of expected future inflation.

14. Surveys of consumers, Reuters/University of Michigan, www.reuters.com/universitymichigan.

15. Survey of Professional Forecasters, Federal Reserve Bank of Philadelphia, www.philadelphiafed.org.

16. Phil Izzo, "The U.S. Economy Hasn't Hit Bottom, Survey Says," *Wall Street Journal*, April 10, 2008.

17. Stephen Roach, "An Open Letter to Ben Bernanke," Global Economic Forum, www.morganstanley.com, July 11, 2006.

18. Ben S. Bernanke, "Outlook of the U.S. Economy," testimony before the Joint Economic Committee, U.S. Congress, April 27, 2006.

19. Greg Robb, "Bernanke Lays Groundwork for a Pause in Rate Hikes," MarketWatch, April 27, 2006.

20. Ethan Harris, "Data Dependent," *Lehman Brothers Global Weekly Economic Monitor*, April 28, 2006.

21. Ben S. Bernanke, "Panel Discussion: Comments on the Outlook for the U.S. Economy and Monetary Policy," speech at the International Monetary Conference, Washington, DC, June 5, 2006.

22. Nell Henderson, "Fed Chief Calls His Remarks A Mistake Talk With Anchor a 'Lapse in Judgment'" *Washington Post*, May 24, 2006.

23. Ethan Harris, "A Bridge over Troubled Waters," *Lehman Brothers Global Weekly Economic Monitor*, September 21, 2007.

24. Ibid.

25. Paul Krugman, "The Greenspan Succession," *New York Times*, January 25, 2005.

26. Meltzer, "That '70s Show."

27. Alan Greenspan, *The Age of Turbulence: Adventures in a New World* (New York: Penguin Press, 2007), 479.

28. Ibid., 483.

29. Ibid.

30. Ibid. 478–479.

31. Ethan Harris, "Neutral Sound Bites," *Lehman Brothers Global Weekly Economic Monitor*, February 18, 2005.

32. Ibid.

33. The idea that Bernanke was being excessively influenced by the markets is more plausible. Of course, he was also criticized for being too insensitive to the markets.

34. Edmund L. Andrews, "Fed Official Moves Up and Into Politics," *New York Times*, June 17, 2005.

35. Ibid.

36. Lowenstein, "The Education of Ben Bernanke."

37. Ben S. Bernanke, "The Transition from Academic to Policymaker," remarks at the Annual Meeting of the American Economic Association, Philadelphia, PA, January 7, 2005.

38. This sounds too low, but the math is clear: in 2006 the United States imported $288 billion from China and about 70 percent of the imports were consumer products. This compares to $9,224 billion in overall consumption and $5,488 billion in services consumption.

39. Steven B. Kaman, Mario Marazzi, and John W. Schindler, "Is China Exporting Deflation?" Federal Reserve Board International Finance Discussion Papers, no. 2004–2791. January 2004. Also see speeches by two FOMC members: Janet Yellen, "Monetary Policy in a Global Environment," May 27, 2006; and Frederic Mishkin, "Globalization, Macroeconomic Performance and Monetary Policy," September 27, 2007. For an outside perspective, see "How Has Globalization Affected Inflation," *IMF World Economic Outlook*, April 2006, www.imf.org.

40. Ben S. Bernanke, remarks from panel discussion "What Have We Learned Since October 1979?" Conference on Reflections on Monetary Policy 25 Years after October 1979, Federal Reserve Bank of St. Louis, St. Louis, MO, October 8, 2004.

Conclusion

1. These acted like putting a lid on a pot of boiling water—suppressing inflation temporarily, but causing an explosion of price increase when the lid was removed.

2. Personal e-mail to author.

3. Gary H. Stern, "Issues in Macroeconomic Policy," remarks to the European Economics and Financial Centre, London, March 27, 2008.

4. Ben S. Bernanke, "Asset-Price 'Bubbles' and Monetary Policy," speech before the New York Chapter of the National Association for Business Economics, New York, October 15, 2002.

5. Ibid.

6. Alan Greenspan, *The Age of Turbulence: Adventures in a New World* (New York: Penguin Press, 2007), 479.

7. Joseph L. Mankiewicz, *All About Eve*, screenplay.

Index

About the Author

Ethan S. Harris is Managing Director and Chief U.S. Economist at Lehman Brothers in New York. In 2006 his team earned the number-one ranking among economists for the fixed-income *Institutional Investor* poll, and in 2007 his team had the most accurate forecast according to a *Wall Street Journal* poll of economists. Prior to joining Lehman Brothers, he worked for nine years at the Federal Reserve Bank of New York. At the Bank he served as the research officer in charge of the Domestic Division and as the assistant to the president of the Bank. He also worked for several years as an international economist at JPMorgan. Mr. Harris has a PhD in economics from Columbia University and a BA in economics from Clark University.